a manual for group facilitators

By

Brian Auvine
Betsy Densmore
Mary Extrom
Scott Poole
Michael Shanklin

Cover by Lindsay McGowen

Illustrations by John Dallman
(unless otherwise credited)

A publication of:

The Center for Conflict Resolution
731 State Street
Madison, WI 53703

(608) 255-0479

A MANUAL FOR GROUP FACILITATORS

First printed March, 1977

Printed in the United States of America

ACKNOWLEDGEMENTS

We want to thank the many people who read the early drafts of this manual and offered comments and suggestions, in particular Ken Weisman, Peter Field, Scott Beadenkopf, Chuck Esser, Elizabeth Nall, Jim Struve, Gary Smith and Gary Brunk. Thanks also to Susan Mattes who helped us in the early stages of this work. We received many helpful suggestions for which we are grateful, both for the ones we incorporated into the manual, and for the ones we were unable to use. We take final responsibility for the way anyone's ideas may appear in this final version.

We are also grateful to the staff of the Wisconsin Substance Abuse Clearinghouse, especially Rich Yoast, for their guidance, encouragement and support.

In addition, we are indebted to R. J. House for allowing us to include his Ugli Orange Exercise in the appendix.

And finally, we want to thank the rest of the staff of the Center for Conflict Resolution for their patience and help during the year and a half that we spent preparing this manual. Particular thanks to Lonnie Weiss, Joe Folger and Jan Kinsolving for their helpful criticism.

TABLE OF CONTENTS

PREFACE

This manual was written in order to share with others some of the information and skills that we, members of the Center for Conflict Resolution, have been developing over the past seven years. The Center for Conflict Resolution is a non-profit, educational organization. Through workshops, consultation, intervention and a resource center we provide information on conflict, group process and problem solving to other groups. We have also sponsored several conferences on peace-related issues and social concerns and have provided training for nonviolent action. Since our inception in 1970 we have been in a constant state of evolution as we attempt--both as a group and as individuals--to find ways of combining education and action in areas of peace and social justice.

Five and a half years ago CCR became a collective, replacing official leaders with facilitators and implementing a consensus decision making process. We began experimenting with this kind of group structure to see how far we could go in sharing the leadership function among all our members and in practicing our values of cooperative and egalitarian group process. Learning to operate as a collective has not always been easy, but it has been rewarding and educational and has vastly improved our ability to help other groups in our function as a skills-sharing center.

Collectives, operating on group concensus, are only one of many possible forms of group structure. We do not feel that every group has to be a collective to use the concepts and skills that we describe in this manual. However, we are convinced that a group is most effective when all its members can participate fully in decision making and group activities. People support what they help to create. Most individuals in leadership roles understand this, but for a variety of reasons, they are often drawn into taking more responsibility than they need to or want to. We have decided to write this manual in order to synthesize all we know about non-directive leadership, which we call facilitation, and to make this information available to others.

This manual is especially addressed to persons who are inexperienced in performing the role of facilitator, but who are called on to act in that capacity. We have particularly focused on a resource person-as-facilitator role--when a person is asked to facilitate a group which is interested in some area of expertise that the person has. However, we expect the information in this manual to be useful to people in a wide variety of group situations in addition to the ones we specifically address.

We do not expect this manual to be the only learning resource for people who are acquiring facilitation skills.
The most important learning resource one can have is
practical experience, particularly the guided experiences
of an actual training course. However, we hope this manual
will be valuable as an introductory survey, as an accompani-
ment to other training, or as a refresher to practicing
facilitators.

The information we present here comes primarily from our
own experience. Although we have drawn on formal education
and published research, everything included in this handbook
also registers as good sense to us and is confirmed by our
experience. We hope to hear from people who read and use
this book. Please send us your comments since we see this
manual as one step in a long process of the development of a
field of information by people practicing these skills.

The five of us who worked together on this manual are--

Brian Auvine: has worked at the Center for Conflict
Resolution and as a research scientist for the University
of Wisconsin for five years.

Betsy Densmore: draws on about eight years of organizational
leadership experience, from political action groups to managing
a restaurant. In addition to working with CCR, she is currently
involved in drug abuse prevention efforts.

Mary Extrom: in her five years' involvement with CCR has
trained individuals in nonviolent direct action and in group
facilitation. Some projects she has worked on involve support
work with Native Americans, a study of racism in education,
and counseling with women.

Scott Poole: has a Master's degree in Communication Arts. He
has worked at CCR for two years and has taught college communi-
cations courses for four years. His interests are organizational
and group communication and techniques of nonviolent social
action.

Michel Shanklin: has been with CCR for a year and a half. She
has worked with community groups for four years, including working with a women's center and crisis counseling.

January 31, 1977

The Center for Conflict Resolution
731 State Street
Madison, Wisconsin 53703

HOW TO USE THIS MANUAL

We want you to be an active user of this manual, a user who will evaluate the material we provide according to your own viewpoint and experience, who will adapt our information to fit your own situation. For this reason we have left wide margins on the pages for you to write notes in, and have written the manual in outline form so that you can locate specific information at the time you need it.

We hope you will read the entire manual, in the order that it is written. However we have attempted to make each section able to stand alone as much as possible. The Table of Contents includes all of the major outline headings and by glancing at it, you can probably find where the information you are looking for is located.

We have tried to present information in a more or less chronological order. Our chapters follow the sequence of preparation, getting started, group process and evaluation. Unfortunately, however, the subject of facilitation does not easily break up into discrete parts. The material in different sections is strongly interdependent and it is not always possible to put each section next to all the other sections that pertain to it. For this reason, the manual contains both redundancy and gaps. If you are reading it straight through, you may notice some repetition of basic points. We feel that this is necessary in order to treat each section fairly. We also feel that certain values and guidelines bear repeating. Even with this repetition, however, we find that many sections require reference to other sections in the manual. We have tried to place these references at the ends of sections where they are easy to locate and don't interfere with the content of that section. If you are familiar with the Table of Contents, you will be in a better position to follow our organization of material.

We strongly urge that all users read the Introduction before reading other parts of the manual. Words such as "facilitation" and "leadership" have different meanings to different people. This first chapter should give you some perspective on where we are coming from, what our values are, and the basic principles on which the rest of the manual is based.

At the front of the manual is a short glossary that includes words (both common and technical) which we use in a specialized sense. This is to let you know exactly what we mean by a certain word which may have different connotations to different people.

We have also included a short bibliography of books which contain exercises. Throughout this manual we will be speaking of exercises, how and when to use them. But, with a few exceptions, we have not included exercises in the text. This is because there are many other good sources of exercises, we are working with a limited amount of space, and we want our readers to be able to find and use a wide variety of exercises, not become dependent on the few that we might recommend.

GLOSSARY

Below is a list of words which we feel need to be defined for the readers of this manual. You will probably find that most of these terms are already familiar to you in some context, but because we use them in a special sense, we feel we should clarify them. These are words which are used frequently in the text, but which, for the most part, are not defined in the text. If a word you are looking for does not appear below, skim the Table of Contents, since we have not included words which appear in a major heading in the manual.

AUTHORITY: Power to direct or influence a group that is derived either from one's role in the group, or from having information that other group members do not have access to.

CLOSURE: A sense of having reached a natural stopping place, a feeling of completion.

CONSENSUS DECISION MAKING (also just CONSENSUS): A decision-making process in which all parties involved explicitly agree to the final decision. Consensus decision making does not mean that all parties are completely satisfied with the final outcome, but that the decision is acceptable to all because no one feels that his or her vital interests or values are violated by it.

CONTENT: The subject of a meeting or discussion, what is being talked about or dealt with.

CUE: An indirect message, often nonverbal, that indicates a certain feeling, desire, or state of mind. Cues are usually unintentional hints, though they may be given on purpose.

EXERCISE: A patterned activity used in a group to promote awareness or learning. Exercises can be used to demonstrate or practice a concept, or to cause the participants to become more aware of themselves or their interactions with others.

EXPECTATIONS: Participants' anticipations about what will happen in a group situation, both what will happen, and the way in which it will happen.

FEEDBACK: A response to a message that tells how the listener perceived the message--how he or she felt about it, interpreted it, or understood it. Also, a similar response to an action.

FREEZE: To limit oneself to a single, narrow mode of behavior or perception, while at the same time failing to see other possible modes.

FOLLOW-UP: To take an action which continues or reinforces some other action or to inquire about the effects of a previous action.

GROUP PROCESS: The means by which group members interact, make decisions, handle problems, and develop roles.

HIDDEN AGENDA: A personal expectation or motivation which can affect how that person behaves in a group or feels about a group, but which is not known to others in the group. A person may have a hidden agenda without being aware of the fact. (For instance, an individual may come to a meeting on "Economic Problems of Cities" because he or she believes energy sources will be discussed. The person may plan to deliberately steer the discussion in that direction, or the person may not even realize that he or she has a private goal not necessarily identical with the group's goal.)

INTERVENE: To take an active role in changing a problem situation, (for example, when a facilitator decides to take an assertive lead in suggesting and implementing solutions in a conflict, as described in "Crisis Intervention.")

NEED: Something which an individual or group feels it must have in order to achieve a sense of well being.

NORM: An accepted and expected model of behavior in a group, or in society.

POWER: The ability to exert influence over a group or over an individual in making decisions, establishing norms, or performing an activity.

PROCESS: See "Group Process"

RESOURCE PERSON: An individual whose role in a group is to provide information on a subject that the group is interested in.

VALUES CLARIFICATION: A process which helps an individual identify his or her basic values. This process often involves using exercises.

Chapter 1

INTRODUCTION:

WHAT WE MEAN BY FACILITATION

We have all had the experience of being involved with other people
in some kind of group that has a particular purpose: Parent Teacher
Associations, church youth groups, bridge clubs, classes in school,
civic committees, family. In some of the groups you have belonged
to, you have probably been called on to fill some kind of leadership
function, whether it be leading a worship service, coordinating a
conference, functioning as a resource person, or being an elected
official in the community. Each of these leadership functions
varies in the formality of the role and in the amount of authority
that the role carries.[1]

There is a wide variety of ways for the functions of leadership to
be performed. Many groups have one person who is designated the
group leader. That person takes responsibility for what occurs in
group gatherings. He or she has been delegated power to take ini-
tiative and responsibility for calling meetings, acting as chairperson, planning agendas and perhaps to make day-to-day decisions
for the group. This is the most common form of group leadership.
An alternative form, however, is for the leadership functions to be
spread throughout the whole group and for all members to share in
these responsibilities. This manual is about how to work with this
kind of group, about how to be a leader in a group where all members
share in decision making and responsibility. The kind of leadership
we will be describing--facilitation--is designed to help make groups
perform more effectively by soliciting the leadership skills and
potential of all members.

The term "facilitation" has been used in different ways by different
people. We use the term to mean a certain kind of role in a group,
which is associated with certain values. In this introductory section, we will define what we mean by "facilitation" and we will
identify the values and responsibilities we attach to this role.
Everything we say in this manual is written from the perspective
that we describe in this first chapter.

I. THE VALUES WE STRESS

   Facilitation, as we describe it, works best when certain values
   are accepted and practiced not only by the facilitator, but by
   the entire group in which facilitation occurs. These values
   are the basis behind the guidelines and suggestions we present
   throughout this manual. As facilitator, it is your responsibility not only to demonstrate these values in your own behavior, but to foster them in the group you are facilitating.

1

A. <u>Democracy</u>: Each person has the opportunity to participate in any group of which he or she is a member without
prejudice; the planning of any meeting is open and shared
by the facilitator and the participants; the agenda is
designed to meet participants' needs and is open to
participant changes; and for the period of time during
which the facilitator is working with the group, no
hierarchical organizational structure is functioning.

B. <u>Responsibility</u>: Each person is responsible for
his or her own life, experiences and behavior. This ex-
tends to taking responsibility for one's participation at
a meeting. As facilitator, you are responsible for the
plans you make, what you do, and how this affects content, participation and process at the session. You are
also responsible for yourself and for what happens to
you. You must be sensitive to how much responsibility
the participants at any meeting are prepared and able to
take. Through experience, participants can learn to take
an increasing amount of responsibility.

C. <u>Cooperation</u>: The facilitator and participants work
<u>together</u> to achieve their collective goals. (One might
say that leadership is something you do <u>to</u> a group;
facilitation is something you do <u>with</u> a group.)

D. <u>Honesty</u>: As facilitator you represent honestly your own
values, feelings, concerns and priorities in working with
a group, and you should set the tone for an expectation
of honesty from all participants. This also means that
you must be honest with the group <u>and</u> with yourself
about what your abilities are. You must represent yourself fairly and not attempt to go beyond your own capa-
bilities in the role of facilitator.

E. <u>Egalitarianism</u>: Each member has something to contribute
to the group and is provided a fair opportunity to do so;
you (the facilitator) understand that you can learn as
much from the participants as they can from you. (At the
same time, any participant has the right to choose <u>not</u> to
participate at any particular point in a meeting.)

II. <u>WHAT A FACILITATOR DOES</u>

Within the kind of group outlined above, a facilitator's job
is to focus on how well people work together. The purpose of
this focus is to insure that members of a group can accomplish
<u>their</u> goals for the meeting. The facilitator trusts that
each member of the group can share responsibility for what
happens, whether it involves calling the members to remind them
of the next meeting, making sure that each person has an opportunity to contribute to a discussion, or seeing that the
agenda serves the group's purpose. The effect of this sharing
can be to equalize the responsibility for the success or
failure of the group (in whatever way that group has defined
its goals and function) and to allow more people to have control in determining what happens within the group and what
decisions are made.

A facilitator can fulfill different kinds of needs in working with a group. This is determined by the group's purpose for coming together and by what is expected of the individual who will act as facilitator. For example, you have been asked to give a presentation on your area of expertise (e.g., regional planning) to a group of interested citizens. The purpose of the gathering is entirely informational. As facilitator-resource person, you can affect the dynamics of the discussion by how you present your information, what kind of atmosphere you set within the group (open vs. closed, light vs. intense) and by the attitude you show toward the people you are working with. A very simple nonverbal cue--where you sit--can affect how comfortable people feel in a discussion following your presentation. If you sit at the front of the room facing the audience which is seated in rows, and have a podium in front of you, you have both a spatial distance and a physical barrier (an object to hide behind) between yourself and the rest of the group. The others are less able to challenge you, and you are protected from hearing what they say. In addition, their attention is focused primarily on you, not on each other. This gives you a great deal of authority. On the other hand, if you can sit among the other participants, with them around you, this will physically equalize the relationships and ease interaction. The purpose of your role as resource person-facilitator is to share information, not to set yourself above the group as an expert. By being open to questions and soliciting feedback, you can accomplish this as well as learn something from the others yourself. This simple example will, we hope, demonstrate a few facets of what facilitation can be like.

One need not be labeled "facilitator" in order to employ facilitation techniques in a group. Any group member can call the group back to the subject of the discussion, interrupt patterns of conflict or misunderstanding between other parties, offer clarifying comments, summarize activities or give evaluative feedback. In some groups, these responsibilities are shared by many or all of the members. Other groups, whose members are less skillful at group process, will expect the facilitator to perform this function alone.

III. CODE OF RESPONSIBILITIES: ETHICS FOR FACILITATORS

There are a number of ways that the role of facilitator can get out of hand or be used unfairly. Often this happens without either the group or the facilitator realizing it. We feel that it is your responsibility to prevent abuse of your position as facilitator. Maintaining your integrity is significantly easier if you have thought through the following code of responsibilities and perhaps discussed them with other facilitators.

A. It is not enough that you yourself have the values of cooperation and egalitarianism. Most people are accustomed to participating in groups where one person acts as leader and where that one person is treated as someone important, someone with special power and wisdom. Unless the group understands your role, they will probably perceive of you as an authority and allow you to influence them unduly. It is important for you to come down off your "pedestal" and let the group see you as "human." This is called <u>demystifying</u> your role as facilitator. Specific techniques for doing this will be described in Chapter Three.

B. Even though you conscientiously demystify your position, however, you may find that people depend on you. They may concede some of their power as participants to you and look to you to make decisions, define a situation, etc. <u>This is probably the strongest test of your own values-- whether you accept and use this power, or whether you reflect back to the group their need to take responsibility</u> for decisions and definitions. The temptation to use the power delegated to you to fill your own needs (increased self-esteem, manipulation of a situation for your own benefit, even simple expedience) will be strong. The fact that the group delegated the power to you is no excuse.

C. A similar potential for abuse rises out of the fact that the facilitator performs a subtle, non-directive role. The passive, friendly, well-meaning facilitator can be manipulative in ways that an aggressive, forceful leader could never get away with. The difference between a charming manipulator and a domineering dictator may only be a matter of whether or not the group is conscious that they are being controlled by their leader. <u>It is your responsibility not to use facilitation techniques to control a group.</u> This is especially true for group participants, not in any open leadership role, who are using these techniques during a meeting.

D. There are no external standards by which facilitators are rated. Anyone can call him- or herself a "facilitator," and this does not necessarily reflect on a person's experience, skills, or understanding of group process. Unfortunately, there are some people who call themselves facilitators, charge groups high fees, and leave them with nothing of lasting value. We hope that the readers of this manual will <u>use the information we present to become more effective in helping groups work well and in sharing skills with others, not for personal profit.</u>

E. Being a facilitator does not mean that you are qualified to be a psychotherapist, either with a group of people or in a one-to-one situation. Because of the stress on human values and feelings that facilitation involves, facilitators are often seen as resources for personal psychological problems as well as for organizational problems. So participants sometimes reach out to facilitators, either directly or indirectly, with their emotional needs. This reaching out can be interpreted as a statement on the lack of resources available for people's problems rather than as a comment on your skills as a therapist. Please be careful.

F. Also, please remember that you, as facilitator, cannot expect that you will meet your own emotional needs working with groups. If you are using a facilitation situation to to satisfy some personal desire (need for attention, respect, power, making friends, finding lovers) you cannot be doing a good job of meeting the group's needs. Often in groups people develop one-sided perceptions of each other, resulting in intense interactions. If you, as facilitator, become particularly involved with one participant (or a small group of participants) you may neglect others, may be seen as an advocate of the one(s) you are involved with. This can be detrimental to the whole group. If you discover a particular attraction, follow it up on your own time.

G. Finally, it is the facilitator's responsibility to be sure the group understands what you are doing with them: what your goals are, how you expect to meet their needs, what you can give them and how you are going to do it. It is your responsibility to represent yourself fairly, to be open to criticism from the group (you are there for their benefit), and to consider altering your own goals to meet the group's goals. It is the group's right to hold you accountable for what you do with them.

All of the material introduced in this first chapter will be expanded in the following chapters. You will notice that much of what we carefully detail in these chapters is simple common sense. One of the purposes of this manual is to help you use the basic human skills and common sense knowledge you already have in working with groups. From time to time we will exhort you to use your intuition. This does not always mean taking the easy way out or pursuing the most comfortable direction. As you gain experience in facilitation, you will learn to trust an inner sense of direction in determining the best behavior in a particular situation based on humane values and an understanding of humans as individuals and in groups, whether this behavior is comfortable or awkward, pleasant or unpleasant, easy or difficult. One does not simply read a book and then become an effective facilitator. You need to combine experience, feedback, observation and reflection in order to develop competence. We have found that experience is the most effective training tool.

As you read, please keep in mind the values and responsibilities described in this chapter. By understanding these concepts, you will understand the basis for guidelines and methods described in the rest of the manual.

IV. SUGGESTED READING

A. Using workshops or group techniques to achieve change:

1. Dorwin Cartwright "Achieving Change in People: Some
    Applications of Group Dynamics Theory" Human Rela-
    tions, 4, 1951, 381-392. OR in R. M. Steers and
    L. W. Porter (eds.) Motivation and Work Bahavior
    (1975: McGraw-Hill) 327-338.

2. Andre Delbecq, Andrew VandeVen and David Gustafson
    Group Techniques for Program Planning (1975: Scott
    Foresman).

3. L. W. Porter, E. E. Lawler III, and J. Richard
    Harkman Behavior in Organizations (1975: McGraw-
    Hill) Chs. 15-17. (This is an excellent introduc-
    tion for the layperson to a wide variety of techniques.)

4. W. G. Bennis, K. B. Benne, and R. Chin The Planning
    of Change (2nd ed.) (1969: Holt).

B. Other manuals on facilitation:

1. Movement for a New Society's Resource Manual for a
    Living Revolution (see page 87 for details).

2. J. William Pfieffer and John E. Jones, eds., Annual
    Handbooks for Group Facilitators (1972 on: Univer-
    sity Associates Publishers, Inc.).

3. A Family Response to the Drug Problem: Group
    Facilitator Guidelines, Dept. Health, Education and
    Welfare (available from the Superintendent of
    Documents, U.S. Government Printing Office, Washington,
    D.C. 20402, Stock No. 017-024-00537-1, for $1.30).
    This is directed to facilitators of groups discussing
    drug problems, but contains useful information for
    any facilitation situation.

Chapter 2

HOMEWORK

This chapter is about the most important thing you can do to insure a good experience for yourself and for the group you will facilitate--preparation. No facilitator, even the most experienced, can expect to do a good job without being thoroughly prepared. By homework, we mean finding out in advance everything you can about the group you will be working with, devising a plan that relates as closely as possible to the needs of the group and the purpose of the session, and checking out your plan with group members to make sure it is what they want. Following are some things to consider as you make your plans.

I. FUNCTIONS OF GROUPS: Groups exist for a variety of purposes and have different methods of pursuing these purposes. It is a good idea to keep the function of the group you will be working with in mind as you make your plans. Some functions of groups are:

    A. Imparting information. A group performing this function emphasizes passing information between group members, or between a resource person and the group. A teacher-classroom relationship is the most typical example of this kind of situation. Facts and theories are stressed.

    B. Skill acquisition. A group concerned with this function emphasizes the acquiring of abilities. While an information imparting group, as described above, would stress the knowledge of theories or techniques, a skills acquisition group focuses on the practical application of this information. An example of this kind of group is a workshop where participants learn and practice new counseling techniques.

    C. Actualization. This group function focuses on the members themselves. It stresses feelings, awareness and self-expression. Consciousness-raising groups and groups practicing values clarification are two examples of actualization.

    D. Setting Objectives. Here the focus is on choice and commitment--on making a decision. The group is choosing among alternatives in order to take a stand, develop a policy, or select a specific direction of action. An example of setting objectives is when a group passes judgment on recommendations of a subcommittee which has emphasized imparting information. Groups which are not primarily objective-setting in their purpose will take on characteristics of this kind of group from time to time when they must determine future goals and strategies.

E. Task performance. A task group is one whose function is
to do a job, whether it be a specific job (develop a new
curriculum for a school) or a general job (increase public understanding of pollution).

You will notice that the first three kinds of functions above
are educational. The fourth kind of function (setting objectives) involves characteristics of both educational and task
groups.

Dividing lines between these five categories are not always
sharp. A group's purpose may vary from meeting to meeting,
or may involve a combination of the above types. For instance, a committee appointed by the mayor to recommend
guidelines for developing youth programs in the city may act
first as an information-imparting group as it studies exist-
ing programs. It may resemble an actualization group when
members try to identify and understand human needs. It is
setting objectives when it selects which needs are most
relevant and what programs are most worth supporting. Finally, it is a task group as it prepares a proposal to return
to the mayor.

As you plan for facilitation, it is valuable to keep in mind
the function of the group you will be working with. This
manual will focus primarily on educational groups (those described under A, B and C above). However, many of the principles we outline will be adaptable to other group situations
as well.

II. SCOUTING: The categories described above are only one of the
many things you will need to look at before you prepare to
facilitate for a group. Below are some questions you can use
as you try to gain a more thorough understanding of the group.

A. Who are the members?

1. How many people are in the group?

2. What are their ages? -- educational/professional
backgrounds? -- sex mix? -- class/culture mix? --
etc.

3. How well informed are they on the topic with which
the group will be dealing?

4. How committed are the members to the goals of the
group? What are their motivations for attending?
(Are they there primarily for self-fulfillment, or
because they are dedicated to achieving the group's
goal?)

5. How voluntary is membership in the group? (Is it a collection of people meeting in their spare time because they want to, or is it a required monthly meeting of department heads?)

6. What do you know about the underlying philosophies that the group shares? (A group of corporate executives will probably share different basic assumptions than a labor union. Nonetheless, you must be careful not to stereotype people on the basis of your assumptions about a group.)

7. How cohesive are the group members? How alike or different are they? How closely do they work together? How well do they understand and trust each other?

B. What is the group's function?

1. How does the group fit into the categories described above under I (Functions of Groups)?

2. What are the group's long range and short range goals?

3. How specific are these goals? (Are they trying to learn more about the effects of poverty, or are they working to repeal City Ordinance H-35.2?)

4. How closely and cooperatively must group members work together to pursue these goals? (Are they representatives of different agencies which get together informally once a month to exchange information about new developments in their field, or do they publish a newsletter with a regular deadline?)

5. What is the purpose of the specific session which you will be attending?

6. Why have you been asked to facilitate? What does the group feel that you have to offer that has caused them to request you?

C. Is it a long term or a short term group?

1. If long term . . .

a. What is the normal structure of the group? How do meetings proceed? How are decisions made?

b. How attentive is the group to members' feelings? How much does the group emphasize understanding and communication?

c. How effective have they been in working toward the group's goals? How satisfied are they with the way they function?

d. What can you find out about intra-group dynamics?
--Who are the leaders?
--What tensions exist?

(This kind of knowledge can be very helpful, but you should be careful not to put too much weight on inside information that you get in advance, since it usually comes from one person's perspective. Consider this information, but try to approach the group with an open mind to whatever interactions may arise.)

2. If short term . . .

a. Review the questions for long term groups. You may be able to get similar information about the members' past group experiences.

b. What are the participants' reasons for being there? What is the circumstance under which the group has been formed?

c. Will the members know each other?

d. How mixed or homogeneous are the backgrounds of the participants? (A public forum will produce a wider variety of people than a professional conference.)

Of course this list is not complete, nor could it be. However, we are trying to point out some of the different angles you may want to pursue in scouting out the group before you facilitate. If the group meets regularly, you may benefit from attending a meeting and seeing them in action first.

The answers to these and similar questions are important in planning. For instance, if the group has a well defined, specific goal, you will want to make plans that are as consistent as possible with this goal. But if the group exists mainly for the fulfillment of its members (such as a consciousness-raising group), your plans can be much more flexible, adaptable to the flow of the session. If you are going to be a resource person presenting information, it is important to know how sophisticated the members' present knowledge of the subject is. Exercises can be planned best when you know how familiar the participants already are with this kind of activity. And you will know in advance that a group that has been meeting for six months will not need to spend much time on introductions, but if the session is a one-time workshop of school administrators from across the state, you will.

The more you know about a group before you plan the session, the better you will be able to prepare yourself to meet their needs and expectations in a way that will be meaningful to them.

III. NEGOTIATING: Once you have been asked to facilitate for a group, you will need to set up a contract, either written or verbal, specifying all the details of the arrangement. Most people prefer to keep things informal and to avoid dealing with too many details. This can be a dangerous practice for facilitators. Very often, when a session flops, it is because the facilitator and group members had different expectations. One of the authors did a workshop on conflict resolution for a training institution. She had been asked to facilitate on short notice and did not have a chance to do much homework. She planned the workshop unaware that the people attending were already familiar with the material she had chosen to present. Only at the end of the workshop, during the evalua- tion, did she find out that the participants had been bored and irritated because they thought she had been talking down to them. If she had had a chance to do adequate homework, she would have been able to plan a format that would have related better to the needs of the participants. It is absolutely essential that you know in advance what the group's needs and expectations are, and that they understand what you plan to do.

Ideally, you will want to negotiate for the session twice.

A. The First Time You Negotiate: In this meeting with the group, or representatives of the group, you get a general idea of what the group is like and what it wants from you. At this point, try to get answers to as many of the ques- tions under II (Scouting) as possible. In addition, you will want such information as:

--How long the session will be.
--Where it will be held (the nature of the environment, the kinds of equipment available).
--If the session is part of a larger program, what group activities will precede and follow it.
--The size of the fee and method of transaction, if you are going to be paid.

Find out as specifically as possible what the group wants. Let them know what you think you can do. Check to see if there are any off-limits areas that you should avoid. Iden- tify any underlying philosophical differences between your- self and the group and see if you can work around them. (If not, perhaps they should consider finding a different facilitator.) If you are trying to accomplish a specific purpose, you might want to plan for some kind of follow-up

to see how well this was achieved. Ask for feedback on
the ideas you have before you plan the agenda.

B. The Second Time You Negotiate: By now you should have
planned your agenda. (It is often helpful to have group
representatives involved in the planning process with
you.) This is when you make sure that your plans are
acceptable and satisfying to them. If they are going to
say "But that's not what we really wanted," the time to
know is now, not halfway through the session. The agenda
you present should be flexible, but not so vague that it
doesn't give the group a good picture of what to expect.

Sometimes it is not possible to negotiate as thoroughly as
we have recommended here. However, the more carefully you
arrange with the group in advance, the more you can expect
to have a smooth session that satisfies both the group and
yourself. When you have made plans through a group representative, it is a good idea to spend a few minutes at the beginning of the session outlining the plans to the whole group
for their understanding and approval--or so that they may
recommend alterations. In long sessions, you should prepare
for the possibility that the group may want to alter the
agenda part way through. This means that your agenda should
be flexible, and that you should present the group with periodic opportunities to give feedback and suggest revisions in
the plans.

We wish to remind you that we strongly recommend using team
facilitation whenever possible. There are a number of reasons
why having two facilitators is preferable to having one. (See
Team Facilitation Techniques, p. 42.)

IV. PLANNING THE SESSION(S): If you have followed our guidelines
so far, you will have laid a good groundwork for making plans.
The most important thing to remember when planning the session
is to know exactly what you want to accomplish and make sure
everything on your agenda logically relates to that goal.

A. Select content that is relevant. The material you use
in the session should be relevant to the purpose of the
meeting and meaningful to the members of the group. Choose
material with the purpose in mind, and modify it so that
it will be useful to the group. Some things you will want
to consider are the backgrounds of the people who are
attending, the time and environment you have to work in,
and your own abilities. If you are going to be providing
new information, think about how to present it so that it
will be meaningful to the participants. Illustrate
points with examples that group members can relate to. A
way to evaluate your material is to try to define exactly
how it will be valuable to group participants. If you
can't come up with anything more than a vague answer, you
should reconsider your material or your method of presenting it.

B. <u>Present materials in a logical order</u>. An exercise concerning interpersonal communication should come side-by-side with a discussion of interpersonal communication, not separated by a film about emotional problems. There should be a logical progression from one agenda item to the next.

C. <u>Plan for time</u>. Once you have an idea of the content of the session, try to determine how long each segment will take. It is a good idea to prepare for the possibility of having too little or too much time. What parts of your agenda can be shortened or left out if time runs short? (If you are prepared for this possibility, you can quickly revise your agenda part way through a meeting if you realize there won't be time for everything.) You should also be prepared with extra material in case things move more quickly than you had planned, or in case you have to leave out part of your agenda for some reason. Extra material can also be useful if the group wants to deal with some subject more in depth than your original agenda provides for. The rule here is to <u>make your agenda flexible</u>.

D. <u>Think about pace</u>. Plan a <u>variety</u> in pace. People will be able to pay attention for longer periods of time if there is an occasional change of pace. Long, long discussions may bore people. Often an exercise will pick things up and give participants something stimulating to spark discussion. On the other hand, too many vigorous activities in a row may wear people out. Some experiences are more valuable when followed by a quiet, reflective period so people can dwell on their meaning. Arrange for regular changes of pace without planning an agenda that jumps from activity to activity so frequently that the tempo becomes choppy and confusing.

If a meeting lasts more than two hours, you should plan a short break. If it lasts for a day or longer, try to plan your agenda so that the logical breaking and transition points fit in with the meal schedules.

E. <u>Use a variety of methods</u>. Remember that people have five senses (at least) and it is a shame to get stuck using only one or two of them. Participants will appreciate variety in methods used for presenting information and sharing ideas. Lectures, diagrams, films, exercises, brainstorming, and other techniques are all valuable, especially when combined. People usually remember more of information they learn in an active way (role playing, discussing) than information they learn in a passive way (reading, listening)[1]. Don't use different techniques <u>just</u> for variety, though. They are most helpful when they truly relate to the subject you are working with.

F. <u>Have a beginning and an ending</u>. Every session should have a <u>beginning</u> in which introductions are made, plans are discussed, and expectations are defined, and an <u>ending</u> which consists of a synthesis or summary of the session and an evaluation to determine how well expectations were met. These will be discussed in more detail below in Chapter Three (Getting Started) and Chapter Six (Evaluation).

G. <u>Nor is the middle a vast wasteland</u>. The way groups function is not a stable plateau between the beginning and the end. Groups go through cycles of social interaction, information seeking, establishing structure and constructive work before they arrive at completion. It is a good idea to have some understanding of these phases as you plan activities and time for the program. Consult Chapter III for a more thorough explanation of group cycles.

Appendix B (p. 75) contains two sample agendas that were developed and used by the authors for workshops we facilitated.

Chapter 3

GETTING STARTED

Your "homework" is completed. All the arrangements are made, and the meeting is about to begin. This chapter provides suggestions, based on our experience, on the things you should do at the beginning of a meeting.

I. <u>BEFORE YOU BEGIN</u>

    A. Take time for yourself to be alone before the session begins. This allows you time to clear your mind, leave your other activities and concerns of the day behind, and focus on the session ahead.

    B. Make sure your agenda is clear in your mind. This will keep you from getting confused once the meeting begins. In addition, if you are familiar with your plans and purposes, you can be more flexible. It will be easier to modify the agenda if this becomes necessary.

II. <u>AS YOU ENTER THE ROOM</u>

The first few moments after participants walk in the door will be important ones in influencing your perceptions of them and their impressions of you. Observe the individuals. You can learn to pick up quite a bit of verbal and nonverbal information which may indicate how well people will work with each other.

  --Are people talking with each other as they walk in? If so, what are they talking about? If not, what kinds of expressions are on their faces.
  --If the participants vary in terms of age, sex or ethnic group, do they mix freely? If not, there could be tensions and miscommunication among them.

It is important for you to be present on time, if not a little early. Even if you have had a chance to work with or observe the group in the past, this will give you an opportunity to pick up on people's moods and feel out the situation on the particular day of the session. It is also a matter of simple courtesy and respect to the group to be on time.

III. <u>SEATING ARRANGEMENTS</u>

In meetings where participants must communicate and cooperate with each other, the seating arrangement can exert a strong influence on group dynamics. It can affect who talks to whom and who is likely to dominate group activities.

A. It is important for each participant to be able to make
eye contact with each of the other participants as much
as possible. (It is especially important for the facilitator to be able to make eye contact with everyone.) A
circle is ideal for this. It lets people look at each
other to the greatest possible extent, thus encouraging
openness and concern in the group. Traditional classroom arrangements with you at the front and everyone
facing you, on the other hand, tend to put you in the
position of authority and separate you from the rest of
the group. Perhaps the most beneficial thing about the
circle is that it puts all members on an equal footing,
as King Arthur realized when he made a giant step forward
in diplomacy by establishing the round table.

B. Tables give people a point of common contact, allow them
to sit comfortably, and provide a place to write and to put
work materials. A disadvantage of tables is that they
restrict movement and sometimes may act as a barrier between people. Tables influence the way group members
interact: people are most likely to talk to those sitting
at right angles to them, next most likely to talk to those
sitting next to them, and much less likely to talk to
those sitting across from them. In addition, whoever is
seated at the head of a rectangular table tends to do more
talking and have a greater influence on the outcome of
the discussion than other members.[1] So, if possible, use
a round or square table. (You can often put two rectangular tables together to make a square.) These shapes allow
group members more eye contact with each other. If you
must use a rectangular table, you should probably sit at
the head of it yourself since you will be more aware of
the advantage of that position and can restrain yourself
from dominating the group.

C. Who sits where: Since people will be more likely to interact with individuals sitting close to themselves, you
may want to ask people not to sit near their close friends
or the people they know best, if a different arrangement
is comfortable for them. This is especially important
in short term groups, or in situations where it is important for many different individuals in the group to interact. By sitting next to people they don't know as well,
group members will be encouraged to get to know others in
the group. This will promote a friendly atmosphere and
help counteract any cliqueishness in the group.

IV. INTRODUCTION

We have found introductions to be very important, both the
facilitator's introduction to the group, and the introduction of group members to you and each other.

A. <u>Your introduction</u>

1. Your introduction should include your credentials--what it is about you that justifies your being there. This is also an opportunity to begin laying groundwork for egalitarian participation, by presenting yourself as a "person" as well as an "expert." According to the situation (whether it is formal or informal, a mood of seriousness or fun) you can make yourself accessible to the participants and let them get to know you.

2. If another person is introducing you, consider how you would like that done. How much detail do you want the introducer to give about you. Would you rather fill in the details yourself?

B. <u>Introduction of the group</u>

1. We strongly recommend that you <u>learn the participants' names</u> as quickly and as best you can. This requires some extra attention, but the group will appreciate it and it will allow you to relate to participants more personally. One way to help yourself to do this is to draw a seating chart with each person's name as participants go around the room introducing themselves. This will allow you to learn names without having to ask each individual for his or her name over and over. Name tags are another good aid, especially when the participants are strangers to each other.

2. Another way to do introductions is to ask people to divide into groups of two or three and talk to each other for a few minutes. Then you go around the room and each person introduces the person he or she talked with in the small group. In a meeting where participants do not know each other already, this method allows everyone to get acquainted with at least one person very quickly, and contributes to a more relaxed, informal session.

3. Introductions can also be used to lead the discussion into the topic of the session. For instance, at a 3-hour workshop on conflict resolution with the local police academy, the authors asked each participant, as part of a self introduction, to describe a conflict he or she had either participated in or observed. This helped relax everybody and allowed us, as facilitators, to gain a sense of the participants' interests and concerns. Other good subjects for this kind of introduction are having people tell why they came to the session, or telling what they already know about the subject.

4. We have also asked participants to share their expectations for the session as they introduced
   themselves. This helps get hidden agendas out into
   the open, helps us decide if we need to modify the
   agenda we have planned, and prevents unfulfilled expectations from being an undercurrent of frustration
   and dissatisfaction throughout the workshop.

V. CLARIFYING ROLES

A. Demystifying the facilitator. Many participants will
   be unfamiliar with facilitation as a leadership style.
   You should make sure everyone in the group understands
   what your role will be. Even with this understanding,
   though, there is likely to be a tendency to treat the
   facilitator as an authority. It is up to you to help
   the group perceive you as "human." Following are some
   ways of achieving this.

   1. Your own attitude towards your skills and resources
      should be a humble one. What you say about facili-
      tation can help people see that you have a combina-
      tion of skills which everyone possesses in some
      degree--that you are in the role of facilitator only
      because you have had an opportunity to develop these
      skills.

   2. Explain the reasoning behind the things you do. If
      you tell why you introduced a particular exercise or
      intervened at a particular point, you are bringing
      your tools and skills down to earth, enabling the
      participants to evaluate them for themselves. This
      leaves you open to criticism or alternative sugges-
      tions. By exposing the logic behind your moves, you
      become more accessible to the group. They understand
      what you hope to accomplish, how your decision making
      works, and that you are not holding anything out on
      them. Thus, they can perceive you as just a person
      who is present to fulfill a need in the group.

   3. Solicit feedback and pay attention to it. Demon-
      strate to the participants that their opinions count.
      Treat their ideas with the same value you do your own.

B. The recorder. Recording, or writing down the content of
   group discussions, is a useful function in many situations.
   The recorder can be either a facilitator (in the case of
   team facilitation) or a group member. In either case,
   participants should understand the purpose of this role
   and how it will be useful to the group. (See p. 41 for
   a more thorough explanation of this technique.)

C. The participants. Egalitarian group participation--
the sharing of leadership responsibilities--may be a
new concept to some or all of the participants. You
may need to take time to tell the group what you expect of them, what their rights and responsibilities
are. You cannot facilitate in a vacuum--it requires
the cooperation of all participants. And, since responsibility for what happens in the group is shared,
the facilitator cannot simply prescribe certain behavior for group members and expect it to be performed.
A group can only function cooperatively when the
members themselves want it to.

D. Altering the roles. Facilitation varies from situation
to situation and your role with one group will not be
the same role you will perform with another group. If
you or the participants are uncomfortable with some
aspect of the facilitator's role (the responsibilities
assigned to it, or your style of performing those responsibilities) then the group should discuss modifying
the role (and the role of participants in relation to
it). This may happen at the beginning of a meeting, or
at some point during its progress.

VI. AGREEING ON PLANS

A. Expectations. It is important to know what the participants' expectations of the session are. This might
be discussed during the introduction, as described on
page 16, or you may want to make it a separate item on
the agenda. In long workshops (especially those lasting several days) we have asked participants to list
their expectations which we would write on a sheet of
newsprint. This was posted where the entire group could
refer to it throughout the session and use it as a basis
for setting goals and making plans. Such a list can
be used during an evaluation period to see if expectations were adequately met.

Even in a short workshop, it is valuable to spend a
little bit of time checking out expectations, even if
it only consists of your saying, "We understand that
you were told that this would be a workshop on some of
the general principles of conflict resolution and that
we would have a lot of group participation and exercises." This gives the group a chance to let you know
how their expectations may differ from what you thought
they were. If expectations are different from what you
had thought, you may be able to accommodate your plans.
If not, at least you will be able to explain the dis-
crepancy to the group at the beginning, which will reduce confusion and frustration.

Very often, when you ask to hear people's expectations, a group will generate a long list of widely varying interests. It is important that you don't give the group the illusion that you have the time or the abilities to meet every one of these expectations. This information is partly for your own use, since it suggests what you might want to emphasize during the meeting, and partly for the group's use, since it gives participants an idea of other members' interests.

B. <u>Agenda review</u>. You should also begin the meeting with an agenda review. Go over the items on the agenda, explain the purpose of each one and the approximate amount of time that it will take. Hopefully the agenda will already have been approved by a group representative--one who was able to speak for the interests of the whole group and not just one or several individuals--but this is the group's chance to decide if the agenda is appropriate for their needs and make suggestions for changes. (Of course you will want to try to accommodate your agenda to any alteration a substantial portion of the group desires, but don't feel obliged to make changes that you are unequipped to handle, or which you feel are unwise for some reason.) An agenda will also give the group a better idea of what is going on during the meeting, the purpose of each activity and were it is leading. We suggest that you post the agenda on newsprint so participants can see it, or else hand out a printed copy.

If, at this time, some members decide they want to leave because the meeting plan is not what they had expected, they should not be censured for doing so. This is a fair and honest reaction, and certainly preferable to having dissatisfied members in the group.

VII. <u>CYCLES GROUPS GO THROUGH</u>

Most groups go through predictable phases in their activities. It is especially important at the beginning of a session to understand these phases since they will affect the pace of the meeting and the dynamics of group interactions. If you understand these phases you will be able to accommodate your agenda to work <u>with</u> them instead of battling <u>against</u> them. Each group behaves differently, of course, but you will be more in tune with what is going on if you can identify the cycle as the group <u>you</u> are working with proceeds. The phases are:

A. <u>Social Interaction</u>. At the beginning of meetings people like to exchange pleasantries that are not related to the group's goal for the meeting. This provides members with an opportunity to identify with each other; it helps people to feel a part of the group, puts them at ease, and serves to unify members for later phases.

B. <u>Information Seeking</u>. This phase helps the group get oriented to its future activities by giving all members as complete an idea as possible of what the group will be doing. In this phase, the group answers the questions who? why? what? and when? in relation to its activities. Agenda review is part of information seeking.

C. <u>Establishing Structure</u>. After the program has been established and the problems that will confront the group characterized, the group must decide what its members will do in pursuing the activity. In some cases, division of labor is appropriate (in a role play, for instance), while in other situations the group may decide that everyone should do the same things (as in brainstorming). Establishing structure in these activities appears simple, but it is often complicated by the fact that participants may be competing for control of the group at this point. This is especially true in newly formed groups. Since people don't yet know each other well and don't have established relations among themselves, they may jockey for control over group procedures or positions in exercises. One way to discourage such contests of power is to get the group to concentrate on the best means for organizing the activity and avoid considering who will "lead" the group or coordinate the exercise. By having participants exchange roles throughout the session, concentration of power or influence by virtue of position in group activities can be minimized. For example, the job of taking notes (which gives a person a certain amount of control in a group) can be switched off every hour.

D. <u>Constructive Work</u>. Here the group does whatever activity it set out to accomplish. How well this phase proceeds is related to how well the previous three stages went. If the previous three were not well covered, there can be problems here. People may have hidden agendas, feel alienated by the group, or not understand what is going on.

E. <u>Completion</u>. Group activities need a natural closing point. Some sort of summary, recommendation, or decision on what to do next should come out of each activity if possible. Without closure, the activity or task may seem meaningless and unsatisfying to group members. Everyone likes a little positive reinforcement, at least.

This cycle is only one of a number of ways to look at group activity. However, we find it especially useful from a facilitation standpoint. When you plan your agenda, keep in mind that the session as a whole will probably go through these phases, and a similar cycle may occur for the specific activities within your agenda. In general, the group will be happier and less frustrated if you don't cut it off in the middle of the cycle and if you can make sure that your activities satisfy all of the phase requirements.

If, in the middle of an exercise or discussion, you observe that the group has jumped back to an earlier phase (usually social interaction), chances are that these phases were not completed adequately. The activity may not be well enough defined, insufficiently structured, or the group may have rushed into the activity without any social interaction phase at all. Hopefully, this chapter on getting started will give you techniques for getting through the early phases. The next chapter (Group Process) will provide information that will be useful in the middle three phases. See Chapter Six (Evaluation) for information on closure. Do not depend too much, however, on a group following these phases exactly. If a phase appears to have been skipped, but the group is functioning well, don't worry.

VIII. GENERAL COMMENTS

We would like to add, at this point, a reminder of some values that we hope you will keep in mind as you facilitate.

As we have suggested ways to begin a session, so too do we want to impress upon you the importance of these first moments when facilitator(s) and participants come together. We know that each individual participates differently and that you, as facilitator, must be open to this. The workshop must be participant oriented rather than facilitator oriented, you must respond to what the participants want rather than imposing what you think is best for them. The latter is a condescending attitude which will get in the way of your being an effective facilitator.

We have found it important to take time in the beginning to do everything we've outlined in this "Getting Started" chapter. Otherwise, misunderstandings can plague the session and stand in the way of learning and sharing.

The introductory period is useful in setting this context for your behavior: that you reserve the right to step into the process when you feel it appropriate (open to the possibility that such an intervention may be inappropriate); that silence is okay; that conflict is okay unless it is destructive to the individuals involved.

The following chapter will continue with the discussion of working with groups as facilitator.

Chapter 4

GROUP PROCESS

This chapter is about working with groups. A group is more than just a collection of individuals. As people work together in groups they share common experiences, good and bad. They develop special jokes, find out each other's sore spots, and work out special sorts of interpersonal relationships among themselves. People often have a special feeling about a group--a feeling of energy or belonging in the group--that is more than their feelings about a collection of strangers or even unacquainted friends. A group is more than any person or set of persons that belong to it. A group has a life of its own.

As you facilitate in a group, you will be aware of the meeting on two levels: <u>content</u> (the subject that is being dealt with) and <u>process</u> (how group members interact). As you prepare your agenda and define expectations with the group, you will be thinking mainly of content. But once the meeting is underway, you will be just as concerned with the process. Your job as facilitator is to help group members work well together, and you should be careful not to let your interest in the content distract you from being aware of <u>how</u> the group is working. Generally, the more you are in tune with <u>yourself</u>, the better you will be able to facilitate. That is because to facilitate well, you must be able to focus your attention outward to the group and not worry about "proving" yourself or protecting your ego. Below we outline some of the things you should be aware of to help a group function well. We encourage you to pass on these group process skills to the groups you work with: giving members skills they can use themselves is your best opportunity to leave them with something of lasting value.

In this chapter, we include some general information that will be useful to you in understanding what is happening in groups you facilitate--information on communication and group dynamics. We will also be describing techniques for using this information as you facilitate--how to phrase questions, facilitate a discussion, and use exercises. These are techniques you will use at any time in any group. In the next chapter we will describe special techniques that you will use in certain situations.

I. <u>COMMUNICATION</u>

Communication is the essential ingredient of any group--like the cement in a brick wall. Your effectiveness as a facilitator depends on your ability to communicate well with the group and to help the group members communicate well with each other. The ability to communicate effectively is a skill, and like any skill, it is best acquired through practice and self-criticism. Following is a list of rules and strategies that are conducive to effective communication. Like all the material covered in this chapter, these rules

are not only guidelines for the facilitator, but may also
be useful material to present in a workshop. Facilitators
aren't the only people who have to communicate.

A. Adapt to your listeners. Something that seems perfectly
clear to you may have an entirely different meaning, or
may be completely incomprehensible to the person you are
talking to. Other people have had different experiences
than you. As a result, they may attach different meanings to words, gestures and appearances than you intend.
To minimize this possibility, adapt:

1. Your language. Make sure that the terms you use are
common usage for the group. Don't use any technical
terms, or jargon familiar to a certain profession or
area of study, without making sure that all the group
agrees on the meaning. A misunderstanding at a recent meeting we attended made the authors realize
that the word "intervention" had an entirely different meaning for a person with a background in labor
negotiation than it did for other group members who
were accustomed to working with collectives. Slang
that is common to your peer group may make others of
different ages, professions, or even geographical
origins, feel uncomfortable, either because it is
offensive to them, or because it is unfamiliar.

2. Your style. The way you dress, carry yourself, and
interact with others will affect how well you fit in
with a group. At a meeting of college students, for
instance, you may want to be very informal. You may
wear blue jeans, sit on the floor, and laugh a lot.
But at a meeting of retired teachers, you may wear
"good clothes," stand up, and tell fewer or different
kinds of jokes. In general, if you are informal and
comfortable with the group, it helps to make them
relax as well. But interpret the word "informal" to
be consistent with the norms of the group. Don't
dress or act in ways that give a false impression,
but do try to avoid turning people off by appearing
strange or threatening in any way.

B. Listening is important. We have all heard the importance
of listening stressed over and over, but listening is
much more difficult than most people realize. Much of
the time when someone is talking to us, we aren't really
listening; we are thinking about what we are going to
say in answer. When you are listening to someone, try
not to immediately evaluate what is being said in terms
of what it means to you; instead, try to understand what
it means from the other person's perspective. Ask questions that will help you understand better what the other
person is thinking and feeling. Not only will you understand better, but you will be able to give an answer that
has meaning to the other, from her or his point of view.

The following exercise will help you become more aware of listening skills:

> List 5 or 6 controversial topics on a piece of paper. You and one other person sit and discuss them. After each person makes a position statement, the other person should try to summarize what the first said. The first person then tells the second whether the summary was accurate. Feedback will indicate how well both parties listen. Often, having a third person observe this exercise and comment afterwards helps. (It is harder than you think!)

C. Be aware of what is happening in the group. Various verbal and nonverbal cues tip you off as to how the people you are talking to are reacting. You can adjust your style (by speaking faster, slower, on a more or less complicated level, by encouraging more or less group participation) or you can check out your interpretation of these cues with the group and get them to suggest revisions in your method. Some cues to watch for are:

1. Restlessness. Are people shifting around a lot? Are they clearing their throats or having side conversations? If so, you are probably losing them. You may be boring them or talking over their heads, or it may be simple fatigue.

2. When silences occur, do they seem comfortable or uncomfortable? In a tense group, silences can be agonizing. If this is the case, several things could be happening: people may be bored because you're going too slow or because your material is too simple; people may be uncomfortable with the topic; or people may be shy with each other and too self-conscious to talk in front of the group.

3. Do people look at you when you talk? If so, they probably feel comfortable with you and are intrigued by what you are saying. If they avoid eye contact, something may be wrong.

4. Do people look at each other when they talk? Again, if they do not avoid one another's gaze, it is a sign that the group is relaxed and at ease. If two or more people won't look at each other, or if two or more people will not talk to each other, there may be something wrong.

5. Postures of group members. People often lean forward and shift positions when they want to say something. Posture can also reflect tension or how relaxed a person is in the group. Naturally, posture also reflects how tired or alert people are as well.

None of these cues can tell you absolutely what is
going on. You must be aware of the situation in which
they are given to even begin to interpret them. Even
more importantly, you must know the individuals pretty
well before you can interpret their cues with assur-
ance. Not everyone reacts in the ways described above.
These cues are listed only to serve as general indicators for you to watch for; check out your interpretation of people's cues with them (see below).

See Chapter Seven for hints on dealing with specific
problems that you might detect from participants'
cues.

D. Test assumptions. Communication and interpersonal
relationships are based on assumptions that people make
about each other and about the relationship. Sometimes
these assumptions are correct, but often they are only
partly correct, or altogether incorrect. People generally believe that their assumptions are correct until
something happens to make them change the assumption.
Sooner or later, most mistaken assumptions lead to a
misunderstanding of one kind or another. The longer a
mistaken assumption has been held, the greater the
problems that such a misunderstanding can bring. For
instance, I may assume that you consider me a close
friend and trust me because every Wednesday afternoon we
have beer together and you tell me about your problems.
This assumption may be correct, or you may just consider
me a pleasant person to kill time with while you are
waiting for your ride home. In the latter case, my feelings may be deeply hurt if I find out that you haven't
told me about something important that is happening in
your life: my assumption that you trust me will be
contradicted. The longer the history of our Wednesday-
beer-relationship, the more betrayed I will feel.

It is impossible to eliminate assumptions from our relationships. Human beings cannot avoid making assumptions.
However, we can minimize the problems that mistaken assumptions can cause. The way to do this is to be aware
of the assumptions you are making, and check them out.
If you feel like group members are too exhausted to continue a session, don't just break the group up. Ask
them if they are tired, or if they want to go on.

One kind of assumption is reflected in words like "always"
and "never." When you say "Sara is always late to meetings," or "Bill never disagrees with Ed" you are assuming that these people are inflexible, that they cannot or
will not change. Nobody always behaves the same way.
When you use such words, you are being unfair to the
people you are speaking about (and they will probably
resent it) and you are being unfair to yourself by limiting the possibilities that you can conceive of.

E. <u>Give feedback</u>. A good way to test assumptions is to provide, and ask for, feedback. Ask people what they mean
by a certain word, or tell them how you feel about what
they just said. This will allow them to explain where
they are coming from, and will let them know how you
feel. Feedback is best if it is given immediately, since
looking back to something that happened two weeks ago is
hard for people. Feedback statements are more helpful if
they are:

1. <u>Specific</u> rather than general: "You bumped my arm"
   rather than "You never watch where you are going."

2. <u>Tentative</u> rather than absolute: "You <u>seem</u> unconcerned
   about this problem" rather than "You don't care what
   happens."

3. <u>Informing</u> rather than commanding: "I haven't finished
   yet" rather than "Stop interrupting me."

4. <u>Suggesting</u> rather than directing: "Have you ever considered talking to Tim about the situation?" rather
   than "Go talk to Tim."

5. <u>Tied to behavior</u> rather than abstract: "You complain
   frequently" rather than "You are immature."

Each of these guidelines is designed to allow the other person maximum latitude in the way she or he responds to you.
At the same time, they are designed to produce feedback
that the other person <u>can</u> respond to, rather than vague
judgments that show the other person how you feel, without
giving her or him any idea of how that judgment was made.

F. <u>How you talk patterns how others respond</u>. What you say de-
termines what other people can say back.[1] If you keep your
half of a conversation at a superficial level, most people
you talk to will respond at a superficial level. If you
are open, other people will often respond with openness.
Telling people about yourself and your feelings will encourage them to respond in kind.

1. Leave your own statements open to criticism and qualification by members of the group. You can set the stage
   for this at the beginning of a session by saying something like, "If you think I'm off base at any time during the meeting, don't hesitate to criticize me or call
   me on it. I certainly won't hesitate to tell you what
   I feel." This encourages people to give you feedback
   as well as encouraging the group to criticize itself.

2. Don't make pronouncements on other people. Qualify your opinions as <u>yours</u>. Say "I think . . ." or "It seems to me that . . . ." Make sure people realize you are expressing your feelings or opinions and not making final judgments. Even statements like "It appears . . ." carry the subtle implication that it appears that way to everyone. Speak only for yourself.

3. Show your commitment and concern for what the group is doing. Hopefully, you will have real commitment and concern. You can't fake it. If you aren't telling the truth, you are likely to be found out, and then you will have exhibited bad faith in the group. Be what you are.

Everyone develops a personal style of communicating. It is important to add your individual touches to how you interact with people. In many ways, every conversation is an experiment. You can, and do, learn every time you talk to someone else. The trick is becoming aware of what you learn, and learning to use that awareness.

II. <u>PHRASING QUESTIONS</u>

As a facilitator, you will be asking many questions in the group--to stimulate discussion, to analyze an exercise, to evaluate group progress.[2] Asking questions so that you get useful, constructive answers from an interested group is an art. You will master it mostly through experience, but there are certain things you can do to make your questions clear and stimulating.

A. <u>Avoid leading questions</u>. The best possible question stimulates the group to draw its own conclusions rather than leading them to yours. "How did you feel about this exercise?" is a question with infinite possible answers. "Did the exercise make you feel uncomfortable?" is a question with two possible answers, "yes" and "no." The first question leaves the group free to discuss whatever ideas occur and seem relevant to the members. The second question traps the discussion into a single theme--discomfort. Eliciting a response from the group to match a conclusion you have already made smacks of (and often is) manipulation. It can lead the group to distrust you. However, if group members are reluctant to volunteer comments, or if you particularly want to discuss the subject of discomfort, then state your conclusion <u>as your own</u> and ask the group to respond. You might say, "I sensed that many of you were uncomfortable during the exercise. Was I right?" If the group confirms your assumption, then you can go on to ask <u>why</u> individuals felt uncomfortable.

B. It often helps to <u>phrase questions in a positive manner</u>. Instead of asking "Why won't this plan work?" ask "What problems will we have to overcome if we adopt this plan?" Instead of asking "What went wrong at this meeting?" ask "What things might we have done differently to make this meeting more successful?"

C. Sometimes you may want to <u>prepare questions in advance</u>. This is particularly helpful with exercises since you already have an idea of what to expect and of fruitful areas to ask questions about. In many instances, the questions you ask will be a bridge to a mini-lecture or to a set of concepts you want to draw out of the exercise. In some situations, it is helpful to inform the group what questions you are going to ask in advance. Some hints on preparing questions are:

1. What purpose does the question have? If it doesn't fit in with the purpose of the exercise or the goals of the meeting, you probably shouldn't be asking it. If it does fit in with the purpose, think through what answers you might receive. If the answers you anticipate don't seem very informative or thought-provoking, you are probably asking the wrong question, or asking it in the wrong way. Try again.

2. When you have thought through the question, try it out on your friends. Their reactions (because they aren't planning a meeting) will be a good judge of how valuable your question is.

3. If you know the purpose of your question, ask yourself: Is a general or a very specific type of answer best for this part of the meeting? If you want general answers, or a broad range of responses, phrase the inquiry in general terms, using abstract words and short questions such as "How did you feel about that exercise?" If you want specific answers, ask specific, detailed questions. For example, instead of the above question, you might ask, "What did you think during the part of the role play where Jim told Louise about his dying mother?"

III. <u>FACILITATING DISCUSSIONS</u>

Your role as facilitator in a discussion will vary according to the kind of discussion and the kind of group you are working with. In some situations you will be a contributing member of the group as well as facilitator; in other situations it will be inappropriate for you to do much venting of your own thoughts and feelings. Sometimes you will be a resource person; at other times group members will know more about the subject being discussed than you. In most discussions, however, the facilitator's job includes <u>keeping the discussion focused</u> on the topic, <u>clarifying</u> (or asking for clarification) when something seems confusing, and helping create and <u>maintain a situation where everyone can participate in a cooperative manner</u>.

A. <u>Getting things rolling</u>. Some discussions don't need stimulating--they happen by themselves. In many cases, however, you will need to help the discussion get started. Following are some principles and techniques that will be helpful.

1. Everyone should <u>know exactly what the discussion is about</u>, and <u>what the reason for having it is</u>. If a discussion is not getting off the ground, if there are awkward silences where everyone looks around the room, waiting for someone else to say something, it could be because members don't know for sure what they are supposed to be talking about, or how to approach the subject.

2. <u>Give participants room to be involved</u>. Being too directive in your role as facilitator may cause others to hesitate to take responsibility for what happens in the group. They may wait for you to provide all the guidance. If it seems that this is happening, make your style more low key.

3. <u>Be a model</u>. Your own behavior can demonstrate to members how they can participate. If the discussion is supposed to be one in which participants relate the problem of discrimination to their own lives, it may help if you demonstrate how the members might approach the subject by describing an incident in which you experienced or witnessed discrimination. Other members of the group may follow your example and pick up the discussion from there. You can help to set a relaxed, open, conversational tone for the discussion by being relaxed, open and conversational yourself during the meeting.

4. <u>Use questions to stimulate discussion</u>. A simple question such as "How do you feel about this problem?" is a good way to start a discussion. See the previous section on phrasing questions for ideas on how to do this.

5. <u>Listing</u> is a technique to generate ideas or approaches that may be used as the basis for the discussion. At a workshop on drug abuse, for instance, you may begin by having the participants brainstorm a list of reasons why people abuse drugs.

6. <u>Going around the room</u> and asking each person for a response is a version of listing. We frequently begin conflict resolution workshops by asking each participant to describe a recent conflict experience.

7. <u>Write things down</u>. During any discussion, and especially when listing, have a recorder (yourself, your team facilitator, or a group member) write each item on a blackboard or sheet of newsprint taped to the wall, so everyone can see what material has been generated and refer to it at will. This list can also be used as a basis for further discussion. For instance, once a group has generated a list of problems, they can look at the written list to break these problems down into general categories. Even when the list isn't on the wall for everyone to see it is often useful to have a recorder to provide the group with a written description of what has happened in a meeting. (See p. 41 for a description of the recorder's role.)

8. <u>Relate the discussion to people's immediate experiences</u>. It is difficult for people to feel very involved in a discussion that is highly abstract or far removed from their own experiences. The more a discussion relates to people's real experiences and concerns, the more enthusiastically they will participate.

9. <u>Use humor</u> to break tension or boredom. Sometimes if you say something preposterous or do something unexpected you can catch the imaginations of people whose minds have wandered or loosen up a formal situation so that hesitant members will feel more comfortable about contributing. Different groups will react in different ways to various kinds of humor. You should know the group you are working with enough to guage their reaction before you do anything kooky.

10. <u>Use your intuition</u> in choosing what techniques to use with any particular group. Each situation will be different. As you gain experience facilitating, you will learn to adapt your style according to the group you are working with.

B. <u>Facilitating during the discussion</u>. There are many things that a facilitator can do to help along a group discussion. What you do will depend on your abilities, your style, the particular group and the particular situation. Sometimes your concern will be primarily with the <u>content</u> of the discussion, sometimes with the <u>interactions</u> between group members (process), most often both. Following are some general categories of facilitator behavior.

1. <u>Equalizing participation</u>. It is not realistic to assume that participation will be divided equally among all group members. Some will <u>want</u> to participate more or less than others. But you can try to keep one person or a small group of people from dominating the discussion and you can provide opportunities for silent members to contribute if they seem interested but can't break into the discussion.

2. <u>Keeping on the subject</u>. Your role may include reminding the group when the discussion is straying off the subject or when the meeting is violating an agenda that was agreed on at the beginning.

3. <u>Clarifying and interpreting</u>. At times you may rephrase something that has been said to make it clearer, or you may interpret what it means to you, personally, or what you think it means to the group. Do this in a tentative way that leaves room for others' viewpoints. Often, instead of doing the clarifying or interpreting yourself, you will want to suggest that another member give feedback on something that was said.

4. <u>Summarizing</u>. This means pulling together various parts of the discussion and summing them up. It includes stating what progress you think has been made, where you think the group is going.

5. <u>Pacemaking</u>. It may also be your role to keep the group aware of how it is proceeding and when it may be time to move on. This includes saying things like, "Has this subject been thoroughly covered? Perhaps we should start talking about how we are going to use this information," or "It looks like we understand each other's viewpoints well enough. I think we are ready to make a decision."

6. <u>"Processing."</u> This means helping the group members work well together on an interpersonal level. This is often the <u>most important part</u> of the facilitator's role. Depending on the group's norms you may do this in many ways. In a group that is alert to its own internal dynamics, you may give direct feedback to members about their interpersonal behavior, or offer diagnostic comments about the dynamics of the group. This would include remarks like, "I get the feeling that the argument here isn't really about the decisions John has made, but about the fact that he has more authority than some of you feel one person should have."

   More often, your function in processing will be to keep communication open between members so that cooperation can occur and conflict can be dealt with constructively. You may do this by providing members with opportunities to express and hear each other's feelings ("Deb, how do <u>you</u> feel about what Gary and Linda have been saying?"), by asking for group feedback ("Does anyone else have an interpretation of what this problem means to the group?"), or by providing suggestions ("It seems to me we're really bogged down. Why don't we break for lunch now and see if we can come back to the question later and get some fresh insights?").

As you engage in any of the behaviors described above, it is important that the group understand that <u>the facilitator's word is not law</u>. Any interpretation or suggestion you make is subject to qualification by other participants. Furthermore, none of these behaviors is restricted to the facilitator. The more accepting the group is of the idea that <u>all</u> members are responsible for what is happening at the session, the more these behaviors will be demonstrated by all group members from time to time.

IV. <u>GROUP DYNAMICS</u>

Group dynamics concerns how people in groups work together. Just as there are certain communication rules that will make you more effective as a facilitator, there are facts and rules about group dynamics that will help you set up a group to work more smoothy and to make your job as facilitator easier. We have already presented some information on group dynamics in Chapter Three (Getting Started) under the headings of Seating Arrangement and Cycles Groups Go Through. In this section we will discuss several other areas of group dynamics that we think will be useful to you.

A. <u>Size of the group</u>. Many experts say five to seven people is the ideal size for a group. Our experience has shown that this is not necessarily true. The "ideal" group size is whatever number the participants feel comfortable with. When a group discusses highly personal matters, three or four people may be the ideal size. On the other hand, when a group of people comes together for the first time, a larger number may be better. CCR held a series of workshops, open to the public, in which social values were the topic of discussion. We found that participants seemed more comfortable and willing to speak out in larger groups (up to 15 people) than in small groups. The larger groups probably provided more anonymity to people speaking their views in front of strangers, less pressure on individuals to carry on the discussion, and perhaps allowed a wider variety of opinions to be expressed.

If group size is something that you can control, check with the participants in advance to find out what they would prefer. If you are at a meeting where the number of participants seems too large, check with people to see if they are comfortable in the group. Members sometimes feel left out and alienated if the group is too large for them to participate, and alienated participants are not likely to volunteer feedback about the situation. (See p. 64 for suggestions about dealing with groups that are too large or small.)

B. <u>Cooperation vs. competition</u>. The more that people in a group cooperate with each other in activities, the more commitment they feel to the group. In many educational situations, people are forced to compete with each other for recognition or to solve problems. To a large extent this is counterproductive to a constructive group experience. In cooperative groups, people are more positive, friendly and trusting. They are also more motivated to participate and feel that the group's work is more their own product than do people in competitive group situations.[3] For all of these reasons, it is desirable to help establish an environment of group cooperation. There are several ways in which this can be done.

1. When you are setting up expectations with the group, you can stress the importance of cooperation and how much the success of the experience depends on an atmosphere of mutual respect among group members.

2. Involving the group in setting its own course is helpful in encouraging cooperation. Groups are usually much more committed to their activities when they decide themselves what those activities will be.

3. The facilitator's style can do much to encourage a cooperative climate in the group. You can encourage members to take responsibility by refraining from arbitrarily setting things up or making decisions yourself. It is especially important to ask for people's opinions initially, until group members get used to participating.

4. There are a number of exercises you can use which involve cooperative processes such as consensus decision making. These can get the group thinking about cooperation and consensus. On page 87 you will find references for sources of such exercises.

5. Placing a high value on cooperation does not mean that conflict should be totally eliminated. Groups in which some conflict exists are often more creative and productive than totally cohesive groups. Ideally a group will have a balance between friendly cooperation (which helps the members trust each other and work well together) and the freedom to speak out and express disagreement (which promotes interest and the development of new ideas).

C. Leadership. Any time a group engages in difficult or prolonged activities, one or more persons will eventually emerge as informal leaders. (Alternatively, if the group has been established for a long time, formal or informal leaders will probably exist already.) There are several ways that leaders can function:

1. They may serve as a model or example for the group.

2. They may help the group solve problems.

3. They may provide interpersonal smoothing between members.

4. They may make decisions for the group.

When the leader does not overly dominate the group, her or his leadership may be helpful. In fact, in some cases, the leader's influence may help the facilitator establish a rapport with the group. If the leader seems too dominant, though, you should not challenge her or him, since a power struggle would probably have a negative effect on the group. It is better to ask the group how suitable the leader's decisions or actions are. You can do this tactfully with questions like, "Does that suggestion seem okay to you all?" or "Does anyone else have any other ideas?" Hopefully, expectations will be set up so that group members will feel free to interject their opinions at any time.

To detect who the leaders or central people in a group are, look for the following cues:

1. Who talks the most? Whose suggestions are most often accepted by the group?

2. Who do group members look at the most when they are talking?

3. Who are suggestions referred to when they come up? Who is the final arbiter on decisions?

4. Who takes the most responsibility?

D. Scapegoating. Sometimes a group will focus on a particular person to blame group problems on. This process is called scapegoating and can be detrimental in several ways.[5] Scapegoating can be harmful to the individual who is the victim. A great deal of hostility may be directed toward the scapegoat, and it is often more than one person can handle. The scapegoat is often someone who has broken the informal rules or norms of the group. (For instance, in a group where cognitive, logical discussions are emphasized, an individual who talks about feelings may be picked on as a scapegoat.) The punishment meted out to such a person is often unjust and cruel.

As facilitator, it is your responsibility to stress the importance of not punishing someone the group perceives to be out of line. You should stress the importance of treating the matter as a group problem and not focusing on personalities. Get people to discuss why the person did whatever behavior the group is being accusing about, and how the others felt about it.

Scapegoating lets the rest of the group off the hook, allows them to shirk responsibility for problems and puts the blame on something outside themselves. Scapegoating inhibits creative problem solving in the group because it limits the focus of people's thoughts and attentions. Furthermore, scapegoating can give the group a common identity as members unite in freezing their viewpoints on a single common issue--that of blaming someone else for their problems. As facilitator, your role is to help the group face up to its responsibilities. Often you can do this by rephrasing the accusation in more general terms and addressing it as a problem to the group. For example, if someone says that Bill is a hindrance to what the group is doing, you might rephrase the complaint as follows: "The group isn't getting anything done. Such a problem is never a single person's fault, but is always caused by some shortcoming in the way the group operates. How could we redesign our structure so the group will operate more effectively?" It would also be a good idea to get Bill to express his ideas as well, so that the reasons for his behavior are clear.

It is also possible for a group to scapegoat an issue or a situation. Students may unite in blaming the "educational system" for their dissatisfaction and low achievement. This kind of scapegoating is as bad for a group as scapegoating an individual since it also freezes people into a single viewpoint and absolves them of personal responsibility. You should handle this in the same ways that we describe above.

V. RULES FOR USING EXERCISES

Exercises are group activities, usually designed to aid learning and awareness. Exercises can be used to illustrate a concept or demonstrate a specific point, to promote self-awareness, to stimulate thought and discussion, or to train participants in a certain skill. They can also be used to promote cooperation and cohesiveness between group members (teambuilders), to help participants become better acquainted, or to serve as an energizer or ice breaker to get things started or pick the group up when it is bogged down.

Ideas that are only abstract can be brought home and made real to people by use of exercises. Exercises are also a good way for people to learn about themselves. However, exercises are not their own justification for being. As tools, exercises serve a purpose. You should never use exercises just to fill up time or add spice to your agenda. Unless participants can understand a real purpose for doing an exercise, they will feel like they are just playing games and may resent the facilitator for manipulating them. Following are some guidelines to help you use exercises effectively.

A. Think about the group and its needs. Select exercises
    that fit the group and its goals. Be sure you know why
    you are using an exercise and be able to articulate this
    to the group. Don't use an exercise that is inappropriate.

B. Be familiar with the exercise. You should preview it be-
    fore you use it, several times if possible. You should know
    what it accomplishes and how that happens. You should be
    aware of the possible outcomes of the exercise, of the
    different ways it may proceed with different people.

C. Don't get carried away with exercises. Don't present
    people with a battery of activities all designed to make
    pretty much the same point. For instance, if your subject
    is values clarification, you can find dozens of possible
    exercises to use. Choose a variety of these exercises
    and be able to articulate the differences between them,
    and the reasons for each one. Values clarification is
    directional--it helps us towards a goal, but is seldom a
    goal all by itself. This is true of most exercises: they
    are tools serving some higher purpose.

D. Giving instructions is a very important part of using ex-
    ercises. The way you introduce the exercise can make a
    big difference in what the exercise means to people. Your
    instructions should include: explaining the objectives
    of the exercise; describing exactly what the participants
    are supposed to do (incomplete or ambiguous directions are
    the fault of many spoiled exercises); state what the rules
    of the exercise are--this includes saying what it is okay
    for people to do, if participants are likely to keep their
    behavior within boundaries that aren't meant to exist; and
    estimate how much time the exercise will take.

    You should also know what your own role will be during the
    exercise. Are you going to participate, observe, or remove
    yourself from the scene entirely? The way you set the
    exercise up can also determine the mood of the exercise.
    For instance, if a role play is supposed to involve fierce
    competition, you may say something like, "You all can use
    any methods for resolving this conflict that you can think
    of, so long as there isn't any bloodshed."

E. Once the exercise has been acted out, it is important to
    process the experience. This means analyzing what happened,
    finding out what it meant, and how this meaning can be ap-
    plied in real life situations. For an exercise to be use-
    ful, people must be able to relate it to their own day-to-
    day realities. You should ask open ended questions (see
    p. 28) to get people to share their experiences and inter-
    pretations. Some questions you might ask are: What went
    on during the exercise? --Why? --How does the exercise

relate to ideas presented earlier in the meeting?
--What new concepts does the exercise suggest? --Did
the exercise involve particular group dynamics that are
worth discussing? --How was the experience of the ex-
cercise like or different from people's expectations?
--What relevance does the exercise have to people's
personal realities?

F.   Remember that any group member has the right to decline
to participate in any given exercise or activity. It
is one thing to encourage people to participate, to try
to draw them out if shyness or doubt of the value of
their contribution is holding them back, but when a
participant expresses a wish to "sit this one out" she
or he should not be pressured or made to feel bad about
the decision in any way.

If you follow these guidelines, you should be able to use
exercises effectively and the group should profit from them.
However, even the best prepared exercises fall short of their
purpose sometimes. See p. 66 for some hints on what to do
if an exercise fails.   Also, see p. 86 for a short bibliography of exercise references.

VI.   <u>SUGGESTED READING</u>

A.   <u>Communication</u>

1.   Clifford Swenson, <u>Interpersonal Relationships</u> (1973:
Scott Foresman). A special-topics introduction to
communication.

2.   Gerald R. Miller and Mark Steinberg, <u>Between People:
A New Analysis of Interpersonal Communication</u> (1975:
Science Research Associates). This is a more rounded
approach to the subject.

B.   <u>Group Dynamics</u>

A.   Michael Argyle, <u>Social Interaction</u> (1969: Atherton
Press) Chs. VI, VII and X are very concise, yet cover
a lot of ground.

B.   Karl Weick, <u>The Social Psychology of Organizing</u> (1969:
Addison-Wesley).

Chapter 5

SPECIAL TECHNIQUES

This chapter is a continuation of group process. It includes techniques that you will not use with every group, but which are useful in certain situations.

I. <u>FACILITATING FILMS</u>

Films, if used properly, are a valuable educational tool. They can provide visual information in areas where mere verbal description is not adequate. They can provide participants with vicarious experience of situations which would otherwise be totally unfamiliar. However, the success of using a film depends on how it is presented to the group, and how the information from the film is used.

A. Like any other activity, a film should serve a specific purpose in the meeting. The film you select should relate to the purpose of the meeting, and should further the group toward meeting its goals for the session. When selecting a film, you should also consider the audience, its background, perspective and needs.

B. Preview the film before you use it. Compare what it says to what you are trying to accomplish. Will it be believable and sophisticated enough for your audience? Is it didactic, preachy, or full of absolutes? (If it is, it may turn the audience off.) Is it the kind of film that will make people feel involved, or will they just passively watch?

C. <u>Before</u> you show the film, tell the group why they are seeing it. Suggest particular things they may want to watch for.

D. After the film, the experience should be <u>processed</u> (in the same way an exercise must be processed). It is not enough just to have watched a movie. In order for it to be valuable, people should be able to <u>do</u> something with the experience. You can help to get a discussion going by asking opening questions. You can ask <u>cognitive</u> questions about the content of the film, and <u>subjective</u> questions about people's feelings, reactions and interpretations. Depending on the purpose of the film, you can ask questions like: Why did characters behave the way they did? How did individuals in the film function in various roles? What did you like? What impressed you? Did you have any new insights? Have you ever been in a similar situation?

II. THINKING AS A GROUP

There are many reasons why group members might want to work
together to generate a list of ideas. For example, they
might want to try to define all of the factors affecting a
certain situation, possible solutions to a problem, or ways
of applying some new concept or technique. Two methods designed to tap a group's creativity in thinking this way are
brainstorming and nominal group technique.

A. Brainstorming is a common method used in groups to help
    members think of as many ideas as possible. During
    brainstorming the members are encouraged to produce
    ideas as quickly as possible without considering the
    value of the idea. The emphasis is on quantity, not
    quality. No criticism of ideas (your own or anyone
    else's) is permitted since people will feel more free
    to let their imaginations wander and to contribute
    freely if they don't have to worry about what others
    will think of their contributions. Each individual is
    free to make as many suggestions as he or she wishes.
    A recorder writes down every contribution on a black-
    board or sheet of newsprint and participants are en-
    couraged to build on other people's ideas. Very often
    an idea that seems useless or silly will trigger another
    idea that turns out to be very valuable. After brain-
    storming, the group can evaluate the suggestions.

B. Nominal group technique is similar to brainstorming, but
    is designed to encourage every single member to contri-
    bute and to prevent the more forceful members from dom-
    inating the proceedings. The procedure begins with a
    silent period of five to ten minutes during which each
    participant writes down as many ideas as possible on a
    sheet of paper. The ideas should be in response to a
    specific question that the group has agreed on (such as
    "What should be done to improve this agency?"). The
    next step is for participants to take turns reading ideas
    from their lists. This is done by taking turns, each
    member reading only one idea at a time. Participants
    are encouraged to add to their lists at any time during
    this stage, and to build on each other's ideas. A re-
    corder writes the ideas down in the contributors' exact
    words on a list that everyone can see. Members are free
    to pass at any time and may join in again at the next turn.

    Only after every idea has been written down does the
    group discuss them. The group clarifies the ideas and,
    if the contributors agree, combines similar ones. After
    the discussion phase, one way of prioritizing the items
    is for each member to write down the five that he or she
    feels are most important, and then to rank the five.
    The recorder reads each item from the list and adds up
    the points assigned to it. (An item is assigned five
    points for each time it is listed as someone's first pri-
    ority, four points each time it is listed second, etc.)
    In this way the group can determine what values the mem-

bers collectively place on the ideas that have been
suggested, _after_ they have been generated.

(It is especially important that the recorder use the
exact words that the contributor uses to describe an idea.
If wording _must_ be altered, it should only be done with
the permission of the contributor, perhaps by asking such
a question as, "Can you think of a shorter way of saying
that?" See the section on recording below.)

(See the book by Andre Delbecq, referenced at the end of this
chapter, for a more thorough description of nominal groups.)

III. THE RECORDER

The recorder's job is to keep track of what is being said in the
group by writing it down. The notes the recorder takes may be
displayed before the group on a blackboard or large sheet of
paper (newsprint) taped to the wall, or they may be written in
a notebook for group members to refer back to later. Such notes
can be very useful to a group. During a discussion, being able
to see what points have been made can help individuals analyze
what has been contributed so far and build on previous contribu-
tions. It is also helpful for a group that is meeting on a
regular basis to be able to refer back to past discussions and
decisions.

A recorder may be a regular group member who has volunteered
to take on the role, or might be a person whose main purpose
for being present is to fill the recorder's role (such as a
second facilitator). This task should not be assigned or under-
taken lightly, however, since it is not as simple as it appears.
Since is impossible to record every word that is said at a meeting, the recorder must select which details to put down, and
how to do it.

The person who acts as recorder should be skillful at organizing and synthesizing material in a visual form. The recorder
should also have the ability to ask people to clarify their comments without appearing disagreeable or confrontive. Often,
the recorder's requests for clarification are a means of keeping the discussion on the subject. A good recorder has a feel
for when this kind of question will be helpful and consistent
with the group's purposes as opposed to being manipulative
intervention.

The job of taking notes is loaded with a substantial amount of
power since it can influence how the group perceives what it is
doing, which subjects it is dealing with are most important,
and where it appears to be going. It is an abuse of power not
to record ideas that are contrary to your own beliefs. A responsible recorder writes down things that people say in their
original words, or gets permission before changing wording.
Even with the best intentions, paraphrasing may result in altering the original meaning of a statement.

If you are working with a group with which you are unfamiliar, and are asking someone from the group to perform the function of recorder, it is a good idea to spend
a little time explaining this role to the group first.

IV. TEAM FACILITATION TECHNIQUES

Facilitation doesn't have to be a one-person task. In fact,
we strongly recommend having two facilitators when possible.
Team facilitation has many advantages. Two facilitators can
serve different roles in the group and thus help each other
out and provide better service to the group. And since each
facilitator will have a different background and different
perspective, they will have different abilities and respond
differently to various situations in the group. By having
two facilitators, you are increasing the amount of skills that
you are taking into the group.

A. Facilitator-Recorder. One division of labor is to have
    one person act in the regular facilitator's capacity,
    and have the second facilitator act as a recorder. Hav-
    ing a skilled person to act in this role can take some
    of the load off the primary facilitator. In addition,
    the recorder can be of great assistance by providing
    written reinforcement of the meeting's directions and
    goals.

B. Process-Content Role Division. One facilitator may focus
    on the content of the discussion, the cognitive subject
    matter. The second facilitator pays attention to what
    is happening in the group, how people are interacting.
    This division allows for more thorough coverage of the
    two roles of resource person and group facilitator.
    While the content facilitator can focus all of his or
    her attention on presenting information, discussing
    ideas, etc., the process facilitator takes the respon-
    sibility for seeing that a participant who is trying in
    vain to get a word in edgewise gets a chance to speak,
    that when the discussion grows monotonous and some par-
    ticipants seem bored, a change of pace is introduced, etc.

D. Active-Passive. One person plays the traditional facili-
    tator role, while the second person is much more low
    key, identifying with the other participants and provid-
    ing feedback to the facilitator.

These role divisions are not strict, nor are they the only
ones possible. When two people are facilitating, it is
easier to alter your role in the group. One facilitator may
carry the weight for awhile, then the other can pick it up.
If one facilitator becomes involved in a conflict, the second
can provide objective processing. If the group decides to
split in two for part of the meeting, each facilitator can
go with one side. A particular advantage is that the facilitators can provide each other with support, point out to
each other problems that one might not be aware of, and remind each other of things that one might have forgotten, etc.

A danger of team facilitation is that two people coming into a group, knowing each other, the material and their plans, and sharing the same expectations, may deliberately or accidentally manipulate the group. They can play the discussion off each other to lead it in a particular direction; they can reinforce each other's perceptions and thus be less sensitive to group input. Both facilitators should be alert to this possibility in order to avoid it.

Team facilitating with an experienced facilitator is an excellent way to acquire experience and learn about working with groups. We recommend that new facilitators do this whenever possible.

V. CONFLICT RESOLUTION

Conflict will be part of the process of any group unless everyone agrees on everything all of the time (which is very unlikely). Conflict is a necessary and creative dynamic in most relationships; it should be treated as something natural, even useful, since it can force a group to become more aware of the ways in which it works, and thus encourage change and growth. However, when conflict in a group becomes destructive and causes hurt feelings, it can destroy efforts toward a common goal or inhibit participation by members who are afraid to express disagreement, or who fear being misunderstood. Conflict is also destructive when people feel put down for their opinions or feelings. It is not surprising that conflicts--either real or perceived--are usually the basis for groups falling apart. This section is designed to give you some insight into the causes and consequences of conflict.[1]

A. Types of Behavior in Conflict

People in conflict can approach the situation competitively, or they can attempt to cooperate, while still acknowledging the existence of a conflict. When people compete in a conflict, they usually perceive that there will be an outcome in which one side wins and the other loses. If people attempt to approach a conflict cooperatively, they try to find a solution in which both parties can be satisfied. People's behavior in conflict falls into five styles described below:

1. Avoiding occurs when one or both parties withdraw from the conflict situation. They either do not acknowledge the existence of the conflict, or they refuse to deal with it.

2. Smoothing is a style in which the party emphasizes preserving the relationship by emphasizing common interests or areas of agreement and failing to confront areas of disagreement. This is often tantamount to giving in. People using this style of conflict behavior are frequently taken advantage of.

3. <u>Compromising</u> occurs when the parties bargain so that each side obtains part of what it wants and gives up part of what it wants. Sometimes compromising is the best solution that can be found to a problem, but often parties compromise without really examining all the alternatives because they assume in advance that "splitting the difference" is the only acceptable solution.

4. <u>Forcing</u> occurs when one side causes the other to acquiesce, thus getting what it wants at the other's expense.

5. <u>Problem solving</u> involves agreeing to cooperate and attempt to find a solution that will meet the needs of both sides at a level sufficient to avoid feelings of losing. It is a difficult but often rewarding style, based on the (selfish) assumption that cooperation elicits the greatest rewards.

To a great extent, there are value judgments attached to these different styles of conflict behavior. However, no one style is always good or always bad. In various situations different behaviors will be appropriate. When one half the group is determined to proceed with a certain activity, but the other half of the group strongly protests that they want to substitute a different activity, and in the meantime valuable meeting time is being lost in what appears to be a hopeless argument, a <u>compromise</u> may be best, such as squeezing both activities in but in abbreviated form, or splitting into two groups. However, if the disagreement is over fundamental goals of a three-day retreat, and there is much flexibility of time, the group may decide to attempt <u>problem solving</u>. If there is a petty disagreement between two members in a large group which will be meeting for the next two hours, then the members may never see each other again, and if the rest of the group is bored by the disagreement and wants to proceed with the agenda, it may be best to <u>avoid</u> the conflict.

The key to turning a conflict into something constructive to the group is <u>flexibility</u>. Ideally, you should be able to change your style of conflict behavior according to the situation, and you should be able to help the group recognize its style and alter its approach when appropriate. As facilitator, you will have to make judgments about your own responses to conflicts and about others' responses. For example, if there is obviously some disagreement about what the group should do next, you may see group members avoiding (they may cease participating and engage in private conversations that are unrelated to group activity) <u>or</u> you may see a member trying to force the group to go his way by filibustering, cutting off other members when they speak, or by putting down those that disagree with him. Your job is to consider how the group is dealing with the conflict and decide whether you should try to get the members to adapt a different style.

The methods you might use to get participants to change their style of conflict behavior might include giving the group direct feedback about its process by describing how you perceive the situation and perhaps by making suggestions about how they might deal with the conflict differently; or you may want to provide more indirect guidance, for example, by asking some uninvolved members of the group what they think about the situation.

Sometimes, you will be a participant in the conflict yourself. In that case, you must be able to step back and apply these same criteria to yourself, as objectively as possible.

B. Diagnosis. There are many things to consider in seeking solutions to conflict. The main one is to try to discover what must be accomplished for both parties to feel that their needs are being met. Try to sort out the real disagreements from the perceptual disagreements (i.e., differences which parties believe exist because they are based on unfounded assumptions about the other party or about the situation).

The following variables may be helpful in sorting out what kind of problem exists, and in choosing which style(s) of conflict behavior are most appropriate.

1. The characteristics of the parties in conflict. What are their values and objectives? What resources (information, group support, self esteem) do they have for waging or resolving conflict? What are their approaches to conflict?

2. Their prior relationship to one another. What has gone on between them in the past (earlier in this meeting, before the meeting)? What are their attitudes and expectations about each other? What does each think that the other thinks about him or her?

3. The nature of the issue(s) giving rise to the conflict. How does each party see the issue? What effect will "winning" or "losing" the conflict have on each party? Does either party have traditions or beliefs that depend on the conflict?

4. <u>The group environment in which the conflict occurs.</u>
   What interest do others in the group have in the
   conflict and its outcome? Does the situation promote
   or discourage conflict? Are there group norms or
   influences which tend to regulate the conflict? Do
   other group members show irritation or boredom?

5. <u>The strategy and tactics employed by the parties in</u>
   <u>conflict.</u> Are rewarding or punishing tactics stressed?
   What threats are voiced and how are they backed up.
   How legitimate are the two parties to each other?
   How open and accurate is communication between them?

6. <u>What time restrictions are affecting the conflict?</u>
   Do the parties perceive plenty of time in which to
   wage the conflict, or are they under pressure to stop
   using group time for the disagreement?

C. <u>Dealing with the Conflict</u>

1. In our experience, many conflicts are the result of
   poor communication or misunderstandings about goals
   and expectations. For instance, if I say that I believe marijuana should be "decriminalized," you may
   think that I mean I want to see it "legalized," and
   you may believe we have a conflict because you don't
   want to see people smoking it in public. However,
   if you believe that people shouldn't be sent to jail
   for using marijuana, then we actually agree--our
   perceived conflict was over the interpretation of a
   word.

   It is always an asset when people can be frank about
   their assumptions. But since that is often difficult, it helps to remember to ask the question: Are
   there different perceptions in the situation? (Be
   sensitive to the fact that often what is originally
   perceived as a source of conflict, may turn out not
   to be.)

2. Another area to concentrate on in clarifying misunderstanding is goals. Ask: What is each party's
   goal? Is this a conflict between different goals?
   Between different approaches to the same goal? Between two parties' different needs? It cannot be
   stressed enough that conflicts are much easier to
   deal with when people know exactly what their goals
   are, as individuals and as a group. Often a heated
   argument will occur between two parties who are so
   involved in the competition that they fail to realize that both sides are seeking the same end. In
   defining goals for yourself, or for your group, be
   as clear and as precise as you can.

3. Once you have diagnosed a conflict and understand its nature, you will be in a better position to decide what kind of conflict behavior is most appropriate. Sometimes a group encounters a problem which demands serious attention. Sometimes the immediate demands of the situation require you to intervene and impose your own ideas on the problem. (See the Crisis Intervention section below.) When there is a substantial amount of time, and when commitment to the group is high, following a problem solving model can usually produce a satisfactory solution. Problem solving (as opposed to crisis intervention) is a process in which the whole group participates. (See p. 48 for one model of problem solving.)

VI. <u>CRISIS INTERVENTION</u>

A. <u>Deciding whether to intervene</u>. Intense conflict is one of a number of situations which may create a crisis in a group. Sometimes whatever is taking place in the group creates difficulties for some of the members. A particular discussion may remind someone of a painful experience. One individual may become disruptive. Such problems are shared by the whole group, and they are everybody's responsibility. As facilitator, you may want to intervene, but before jumping in, consider your options carefully. Beware of your own biases, and be sure that you aren't about to overreact. Can the problem be dealt with by taking a break, by being patient, by someone else? Does the group appear to perceive the problem? If so, is it making them uncomfortable (tense, uneasy, silent)? Is anyone else doing anything about the situation?

B. <u>Your role in intervention</u>. If a problem has become intense enough to create a blockage in group process, you may decide that intervention is necessary. You might begin by checking out your perceptions with the group and soliciting insight as to what is happening. You may deal with the problem on a <u>content</u> level (i.e., deal with the issue that is the subject of disagreement), or you may deal with it on a <u>process</u> level (i.e., approach the <u>way</u> in which the disagreeing parties are behaving). You should try, as much as possible, to remain objective about the problem, acting as a clarifier and summarizer rather than as a party to the conflict. If you are already involved, it may be best to get someone else to act as facilitator for the time being.

During a crisis, people's feelings are especially important. Allow for expression of feelings, but don't get lost in them. When expressing your feelings becomes an excuse for scapegoating or generalizations ("You never give my ideas a chance!") you have moved away from resolution, and are helping instead to make people more defensive or hurt.

Chapter Seven provides more information for dealing with specific kinds of crises. See, especially, the first paragraph of the chapter (p. 59), "When Arguments Break Out," (p. 63) and "Someone 'Freaks Out'" (p. 70).

VII. PROBLEM SOLVING

Problem solving is a cooperative way of approaching conflict in which the parties attempt to find a solution that satisfies everyone. Problem solving is a valuable process when you have time and when the individuals involved are highly committed to the process. Even when a perfect solution--one that lets everyone get everything they want--cannot be found, problem solving will usually lead you to the best acceptable solution. We will concentrate here on what you can do to make problem solving easier and more likely to work. Although we will be focusing primarily on conflicts between two parties, the techniques we describe can be adapted to situations in which there are more than two parties, as well as to group decision making situations that do not necessarily arise out of conflict. This section will make much more sense to you if you have an understanding of group process skills, so we recommend that you read Chapter Four (especially the sections on Communication and Group Dynamics) and the section in this chapter on Conflict Resolution before you go on.

A. Below are some conditions that should exist before you attempt problem solving for the process to be effective.

1. Both parties must recognize that they have a common problem. One of the most important moves in creating a problem solving situation is getting people to recognize common interests and a common ground for cooperation. A first step in this direction is to get the participants to realize that everyone involved is part of the problem, that neither side is "right" or "wrong," and that both sides must cooperate if the problem is to be solved.

This is easier to achieve if group members share a basic value of equality in the group and if they have a constructive attitude toward conflict. A little beforehand consciousness-raising is one way to promote this. Talk to the group about conflict resolution and problem solving before conflicts arise.

As facilitator, you can influence the group to perceive the conflict as a shared problem in the way you describe the situation. For example, it is better to say "Ken and George seem to have a problem," than "George looks like he's about to knock Ken's head off." The former description takes the heat off George and makes it clear that the problem belongs to both of them.

2. <u>Both parties must perceive a balance in resources</u>. Approval and support from other group members, personal security, influence, popularity, information and intelligence are all resources available to group members for achieving their goals. In conflict situations, they will often employ these resources in their efforts to get their way. Problem solving is more likely to be successful if both sides perceive a balance in their resources.

This is likely to occur if neither side feels favored by the group. Ideally, the group should be supportive of both sides on a personal level, yet not take sides in the conflict. This encourages both parties to deal with the conflict, yet lets them know that, although they are valued personally, they can't expect the group to come to their side if they press their case against the other. This makes the confrontation a fair one.

The facilitator can <u>be a model to the group of equal treatment for all</u>, not just during the conflict, but throughout the session. Point out that the problem is <u>everyone's</u>, that if everyone isn't benefited by the solution, no one will be because the whole group will be undermined.

It is also important to <u>establish open communication and expression of feelings</u> as a norm of the group process. Being able to say whatever is on your mind without fear of ridicule helps to create a feeling of acceptance and balance between people. If the group is nonjudgmental, problem solving will be easier.

Even if the group isn't <u>really</u> supportive (although ideally it will be), it <u>is</u> enough if both sides feel free to express themselves and if one side doesn't have any obvious alliances with other people in the group. The more people that are involved in a problem, the harder it will be to solve.

3. <u>There must be trust and good faith between the parties involved in the conflict</u>. People must talk honestly about the problem and take the problem solving process seriously. This doesn't mean that the parties must be close friends, but they do have to have a feeling of honesty and commitment about the other person. (See the section on communication, p. 23; and "Cooperation vs. Competition," p. 33.)

People are more likely to feel committed to the problem solving process if they <u>chose</u> to problem solve rather than having the process imposed on them by the facilitator. A discussion of the pros and cons of problem solving may promote that. However, do not pressure the group to undertake this process because you consider it appropriate. If members are to problem solve in good faith, they must choose to do so themselves.

4. <u>You must have a lot of time</u>. For problem solving to work well, participants must be free of time restraints. If you don't have plenty of time, there will not be room for problem solving.

5. <u>Threat must be reduced for all involved</u>. If a person feels threatened, then trust, open communication and patience are impossible. Threats close people's eyes and ears to things they would be sensitive to in a calmer situation. One way to reduce threat is to <u>focus on the problem, not on the people</u>. Rephrasing the problem so that it seems objective rather than the fault of one person (as we did for Ken and George) can help relax threatened people. If no one feels blamed, much of the reason for threat will be gone.

B. <u>The Process of Problem Solving</u>

There are a number of recommended approaches to problem solving. This four-step plan can be adapted well to a group situation, and has much in common with other methods. It is important to use an open communication style in problem solving. Questions should be phrased to be open ended, not limiting the way a person can respond. You and the participants should be willing to accept feedback from the others involved. (Calling responses "feedback" instead of "criticism" avoids the negative associations of the latter word.) (Refer to "Communication" p. 23; and "Phrasing Questions" p. 28.) The steps of problem solving are:

1. <u>Testing of perceptions by both parties</u>. People in conflicts are especially prone to make rash assumptions about the opponents. It is especially easy for them to distort facts, assume beliefs or motives of the other party that are not present. (An example of this is the attitude many Americans had about Russians in the 1950's: they weren't really human; they were maniacal Marxist machines out to conquer the world. Anyone who knows even one Russian is aware of how extreme this stereotype is. Russians have many of the same hopes and fears that Americans do, and we have as much in common with them as we have differences.) This is not to imply that <u>every</u>

conflict is due <u>only</u> to lack of communication or that every set of parties in conflict has a broad range of common interests. It does suggest that people must get facts and feelings straight before they can deal with conflict in a clearheaded, creative manner. Some ways of achieving this are:

a. There are a number of exercises that can help groups gain a better understanding of the dynamics involved in conflict. Exercises such as Ugli Orange (see p. 81) can be used to introduce a discussion of conflict behavior and the role of assumptions and communication problems in perpetuating conflict. Other exercises can be used to help people get better acquainted with each other while keying them into stereotypes they hold of their opponents. For example:

  Ask participants to list the characteristics and feelings they think other members of the group might have on the basis of what they already know about them. You might ask questions like: "What are Jane's religious beliefs?" or "How does Fred feel about working in groups?" Then have members show their lists to the person they characterized. The number of errors will portray graphically how little two people can assume they know about each other.

  (Sources of other useful exercises are listed on p. 87.)

b. Encourage one of the parties to exhibit cooperative behavior or point out how they have cooperated previously. This demonstrates the party's commitment to problem solving and willingness to work cooperatively. Some things to point out are: likes or dislikes that the parties have in common; values that they share; goals they have in common; or ways in which one party has received help from the other in the past. (For instance, Tom and Ann may both want the meeting to proceed faster, Tom for reasons of efficiency and Ann because she has other plans. Tom and Ann have a common goal irrespective of their different values and purposes.)

  In general, people tend to like those who have similar beliefs, desires, values and interests.[2] Take advantage of this fact to point out common ground (or even better, get the people involved in the conflict to find the common ground).

The whole purpose behind checking perceptions is to get the people involved to focus on the problem rather than personalities or other people in the group. Even if two people rub each other the wrong way and that seems to be the root of the problem, personal differences can be worked out through creative thinking and commitment in many cases.

2. Analyze the problem in as much detail as possible. The important thing in this phase of the process is to separate analysis of the problem from thinking about solutions, and both of these from the final evaluation. If you start thinking about solutions too soon, you are likely to freeze your thinking process before you get a full picture of the problem. Use these guidelines:

   a. Have people state the problems and goals in as specific a form as possible. (Try to meet a general goal like "have better communication," or solve a general problem like "bad communication" and you will quickly see the merit of making things as specific as possible.)

   b. As much as possible, goals should be stated as common priorities rather than individual wants. By setting goals as general group aims, you avoid having them identified with any person or interest. This allows each goal and problem to be evaluated objectively rather than as a personal interest.

   c. State problems as obstacles rather than in terms of solutions. If someone says, "We need a regular chairperson in this group," you might want to get that person to explain why. Usually the explanation will be a statement of some problem. Thus you can focus on "Meetings proceed inefficiently: nothing ever gets done on time." By stating a problem rather than a need for a particular solution, you avoid getting locked into one track too soon. The group can proceed to suggest a range of solutions for the problem--some of which might be more imaginative and work better than the ready-made chairperson solution.

   d. Out of this phase should come a statement of the problems and a general set of goals which must be met if the problem is to be solved.

3. Generate possible solutions. The emphasis here is on possible. At this point you don't want to begin ruling out any ideas, making any decisions, or evaluating in any way. Generate as many ideas as possible,

letting everyone participate as much as he or she can without doing any evaluating or criticizing as you go along. Judgments at this stage may hamper creativity. People will be hesitant to make suggestions because they will be concerned about whether people will consider their idea "good enough," or whether they will criticize it. At this point you just want to come up with as many ideas as you can.

Two very good techniques for generating possible solutions are brainstorming and the first phases of the nominal group technique. See p. 40 for an explanation of these processes.

4. Evaluation of the solutions. In this phase the various solutions are discussed by the group and one is chosen. The best way to choose a solution is by consensus (unanimous agreement). If you vote, you are forcing a decision on the minority--which is the very opposite of problem solving. Using consensus makes sure that the solution is acceptable to everyone involved.

   a. Evaluate in terms of both quality and acceptability. Use objective criteria as much as possible (i.e., pick those that everyone can agree upon).

   b. Don't require people to justify their choices or feelings. Demanding explanations would increase the possibility of their feeling threatened.

   c. Deal with anger and other feelings as they occur. Don't tell people to suppress feelings until later. Dealing with feelings is an important part of the problem solving process.

   In general, deal with what the group perceives as choices or options by taking a problem-centered approach. When you have a problem to solve, you also have a criterion to evaluate possible choices by. If the group has a problem, turn it into a choice. By putting up several alternative solutions, the problem can often be eliminated in such a way that all people are satisfied.

C. Special Note on "Personality Problems": If you have a true personality problem, there isn't much you can do about it. However, real personality problems are much rarer than people ordinarily assume. A "personality problem" is often a misdiagnosis of other problems that are soluble. For instance, two group members might repeatedly clash, disagreeing with each other at all turns and expressing intense hostility toward each other. At first glance, there is a temptation to write off their arguments as a personality clash. However, probing and careful analysis may reveal that the clash is caused by frustration rising out of contradictory definitions of their different roles in the group. (Linda is expected to make frequent decisions on matters which require information that only Karen has access to.) In other words, the two people are mad at each other, and this anger can make them dislike each other, but it is not a personality clash. The cause of the problem is the group process, and working on the group process can go a long way toward eliminating the personality clash. This is not to say that personality clashes don't occur--sometimes they do. It is to suggest, however, that you should look carefully before you decide what the cause of any problem in a group is. Being in a group where the communication channels are open and people are straightforward makes diagnosing problems easier. Be optimistic about the possibility of solving a problem as long as possible.

VIII. SUGGESTED READING

A. Thinking as a Group

    1. Andre Delbecq, Andrew Van de Ven, and David Gustafson, Group Techniques for Program Planning (1975: Scott-Foresman).

B. Conflict Resolution

    1. Alan Filley, Interpersonal Conflict Resolution (1975: Scott-Foresman). A very good general summary of the area.

    2. Fred Jandt, Conflict Resolution Through Communication (1973: Harper and Row).

C. Problem Solving

    1. W. G. Bennis, Organization Development: Its Nature, Origins and Prospects (1969: Addison-Wesley).

    2. Alan Filley (same as above).

Chapter 6

EVALUATION

At some point, you and the participants will want to stop to consider the process, progress and prognosis of the session.

I. DEFINITION AND FUNCTION

A. An evaluation is time taken out during, or at the end of a meeting, for participants to express how they feel about what has been going on. It may also include discussion of how things might be done differently in the future.

Usually, it is possible for the facilitator to guess how well the session is going from indirect cues from the group such as the level of participation, spontaneous comments, etc. Nonetheless, a formal evaluation is valuable because it gives the facilitator a chance to verify or correct earlier impressions, and it gives other group members an opportunity to share their opinions.

B. The function of an evaluation is:

1. To improve group process by allowing participants to consider past experience and discuss future directions.

2. To allow the group to decide if there is a need for future meetings and/or to plan those meetings.

3. To give participants the opportunity and incentive to express feelings and thoughts they may have held back during earlier parts of the session. This is often the only time some people will feel comfortable enough to express their ideas. Negative comments, especially, are often suppressed because individuals fear they will be disruptive or threatening to the rest of the group. Giving the group specific time and attention for their evaluative comments not only encourages expression of these opinions, but gives the participants the satisfaction of knowing that their viewpoints are being considered. The evaluation period is often a time when earlier, unexpressed misunderstandings between group members, or members and the facilitator, are cleared up.

4. To give a sense of closure to the meeting. Sessions without a final evaluation often seem just to end. People like to review their experiences and pull them all together. An evaluation helps this happen. (In an extended workshop or conference, an evaluation can give a similar sense of closure to one section before the transition to a new activity.)

II. HOW TO HANDLE AN EVALUATION

A. Times for Evaluation

1. Evaluations can occur spontaneously during the course of the meeting. The facilitator should encourage participants to evaluate the content and process of the meeting at periodic transition points, such as the end of a phase on the agenda or after an exercise. Even when a formal evaluation is planned for the end of the meeting, the facilitator should emphasize the importance of in-process evaluation. Glaring problems can be rectified in this way, and more importantly, participants will have a sense of control over what happens. If no spontaneous comments are forthcoming, the facilitator should be prepared with specific questions to elicit reactions, such as how valuable do people feel a certain activity is; are changes in the agenda called for; etc.

2. A formal evaluation should be scheduled for the end of the meeting. At least 15 minutes should be set aside for this purpose at a meeting of a few hours. If the meeting is very long (all day or more than a day), then an hour or more may be necessary for a thorough evaluation, and shorter evaluations should be held at intervals during the meeting.

B. Conducting the Evaluation

1. You can't expect people to know what an evaluation is until you explain it. Most people--even those used to attending meetings--don't consider evaluation as part of the process. So explain what you mean by the term at the beginning of the meeting.

2. Evaluations are best when they are specific. While it is good to hear about people's general impressions (the meeting was good, boring, confused), the most useful information comes from evaluating specific events or exercises and the roles played by various individuals.

3. Forms of evaluation:

   a. An informal discussion , or a discussion based on questions that you pose, is one kind of evaluation. It has the benefit of being spontaneous and it gives you the opportunity of asking for clarification or elaboration of people's comments. You will also have a chance to see what impressions are most meaningful to the participants by observing which subjects they most want to talk about. This kind of evaluation gives the participants a chance to express ideas you may not think to ask for in a written questionnaire, and it gives them a chance to react to each other's comments. Finally, verbal evaluation sessions give group members an opportunity to address comments to each other as well as to the facilitator, and they give the facilitator a chance to make remarks to the group.

b. You may also want to ask for <u>written feedback</u>. The advantages of this are that you will get a response from nearly everyone, and you can get answers to a standard set of questions, if you choose. In addition, you may get some feedback in written form that individuals would prefer not to verbalize.

c. Another option is to have members <u>send in written responses some time after the meeting</u>. You will probably not receive responses from many (or most) of the participants, but those that you do receive will be the longer-lived impressions, rather than immediate reactions.

4. The <u>kinds of questions you ask</u> will help to determine how useful the evaluation responses will be to you. You will want to ask questions that elicit criticism, but which will also help you find out your strong points and which will encourage constructive suggestions about how you might do things differently in the future. Open-ended questions will give people the most freedom in their response. Some sample questions are:

a. What went well and why? What could have been improved?

b. In what ways was the facilitator's role helpful or inhibiting?

c. What specific things do you think you gained out of this session (or discussion or exercise)?

d. If a list of participants' expectations was made at the beginning of the session, you can go back over the list and see how well these expectations were met.

On rare occasions, you may choose to use some closed questions in your evaluation. For instance, if you think you may have a problem with talking too fast, and you want to get a specific response from all participants in this matter, you may present the written question: "Agree-Disagree: The facilitator talked too fast." Or you may be facilitating a workshop for an agency that is contracting a series of workshops. That agency may wish to make an accountability measurement of each workshop by using a standardized questionnaire that includes such items as: "Rank the usefulness of this seminar in relation to your job on a 10-point scale." While such questions have their place, the amount of information they can provide is limited. We recommend that when you must use this kind of format that you always combine it with an informal discussion of the type described above.

For more information, see "Phrasing Questions" p. 28.

5. Remember that the purpose of the evaluation varies between single-session meetings and on-going sessions. Each will require somewhat different questions and emphases. In the latter case, especially, a written copy of comments should be kept for later reference.

III. <u>USE THE EVALUATION TO IMPROVE YOUR FACILITATION THE NEXT TIME</u>

A. <u>You can't expect to please everyone</u>. People come to meetings with different sets of expectations, and these will be widely varied, if not completely at odds with each other. Not even the best facilitator can meet everyone's expectations all of the time. Expect some criticism. In fact, if none is received, you should suspect that the evaluation was not as thorough or as honest as it could have been.

B. <u>Look for patterns in the evaluation</u>. You may think one phase of the meeting went well or poorly. One comment contrary to your own impressions should certainly be considered in light of the reason given for the reaction, but if you receive several contrary comments (whatever the reasoning), you should take a look at why your own impressions could have varied so highly from a substantial portion of the group. Think about how you can try to be more closely in touch with groups you work with in the future.

C. <u>Examine the material you use</u> in light of evaluations you receive. As you obtain experience in different situations, look for new materials and activities to use, or modify old ones according to the feedback you receive. In addition, develop your style of facilitation according to what you learn from people's comments.

D. <u>Consider your own standards</u> as well as participants'. Sometimes you will get negative feedback for doing the right thing. Feedback from group members is your best guide, but your own judgment should carry some weight as well.

Chapter 7

WHAT CAN GO WRONG: WHAT TO DO ABOUT IT

Even under the best of circumstances, certain problems may occur. As the facilitator, if you are aware of problems as they arise and are prepared to deal with them, you can usually prevent them from marring the session. There are a number of things you can do when you recognize that a problem exists. One is to do nothing. It is not always possible or necessary for the facilitator to cure every minor ill that the group suffers. You may decide that a particular problem is not serious and if left alone may disappear or be handled by other members of the group.

However, if you judge that a situation threatens the group's functioning, you may decide to take action in several ways. Discreetly dealing with the problem yourself is sometimes the answer. You might do this by taking the individuals involved aside for a private discussion, by changing your own facilitation style, or by changing the agenda. Other times, it may be best to include the whole group in dealing with the problem. You can often get them to do this by describing how you perceive the situation and/or soliciting others to describe their perceptions. This can encourage some participants to suggest solutions. If no one volunteers a solution, you can ask for suggestions, or you can make suggestions of your own. Sometimes just making the group aware of a problem (such as a discussion getting off track) will be enough to get the problem under control.

Don't let problems frighten you. It is very rare for a group meeting to proceed absolutely perfectly and problems are not necessarily indicators of poor facilitation on your part. The facilitator's job is to be cautious of incipient problems and to help the group control them. Following are descriptions of some classic difficulties and some suggestions for handling them. At the end of the chapter is a summary of general principles that should guide you in preventing and handling problems.

I. WHEN PEOPLE ARE NOT PARTICIPATING OR WHEN THEY APPEAR BORED

  A. Situation one: One or two people (a small fraction of the group) have obviously dropped out of the discussion, apparently from boredom, although the group as a whole appears to be functioning well.

    1. Try to determine for yourself whether this behavior is being disruptive to the rest of the group. (Is the dropout staring quietly into space, or blatantly distracting others?) If the behavior is disruptive, the dropout may be expressing some kind of dissatisfaction with the group that he or she has not felt free or able to verbalize. One way of dealing with this immediately is to ask the dropout if there is any comment he or she would like to

contribute. You are thus offering the person an opportunity to make any criticism that relates to the
disruptive behavior, and allowing the group an opportunity to deal with the problem. This solution
has some potential dangers. One is that the individual involved may feel threatened at being singled
out, even though the disruptive behavior was calling
attention to him or her. Another danger is that the
group may become bogged down discussing the needs or
problems of one person, which may not relate to the
purpose of the meeting. You should try to read the
situation to decide if the problem should be dealt
with openly by the group.

2. If no disruption is involved, and if normal attempts
   to include the dropout in group activity are ineffec-
   tive, it is generally best to wait for a break in
   the meeting and approach the dropout privately to ask
   if he or she is bored or dissatisfied with the meeting.
   Try to do this in a low key, friendly, concerned
   manner not reminiscent of teacher calling the misbe-
   having pupil in after class. A private encounter is
   often (though not always) less threatening and is more
   likely to elicit an honest response. This may also
   prevent a time-consuming digression within the group.
   Often the answer will simply be, "I'm not up for a
   meeting today. I have a lot of other things on my
   mind." You should accept and respect this kind of
   answer. It is not the facilitator's job to force
   everyone to be interested and active in the group if
   there are outside factors preventing this. However,
   if the problem has something to do with the purpose
   or process of the group, the facilitator can bring it
   to the attention of the whole group (perhaps by encouraging the individual to express the concerns involved.)

B. Situation two: The whole group, or a substantial portion,
   is bored or unwilling to participate.

   1. Consider reviewing the group goals that were set up
      at the beginning of the session. People may feel
      that what is happening is irrelevant to their con-
      cerns.

   2. The proceedings may have become too abstract or in-
      tellectual. This may be the time to introduce a
      specific exercise or role play which will bring the
      group back to earth and encourage some expression
      and participation.

   3. The group may feel that the session is wandering,
      that there is no apparent movement toward group
      goals. It is important to preserve a sense of some
      sort of structure and movement within the meeting.
      This is where an agenda or timetable is invaluable.

You should refer to this frequently during the meeting both as a way of reminding the group of its progress and as a way of allowing changes in the schedule if feelings have changed.

4. It may be time for a break. Participants' attention spans can only be expected to last two hours, at the most. When people are tired, hungry, or physically uncomfortable from sitting too long, participation will quickly drop.

5. Interjection of humor or something unexpected into the discussion is a temporary way of drawing interest back into the group. Use it to focus attention on to whatever you suspect the real problem to be.

6. You may be working at too complex or too simple a level. See p. 69.

7. People may be afraid of or intimidated by the facilitator or some other person in the group (e.g., a person with a dominating personality). Directing questions toward the rest of the group in the former case, or asking for someone else to respond in the latter, may help to break down inhibitions and get the conversation moving. You should watch out that you do not respond to everything that is said, nor should you let anyone else do so.

II. WHEN PEOPLE COME DOWN ON THE FACILITATOR

A. (An ounce of prevention is worth . . . .) If you have not set yourself up as leader and prime mover at the beginning of the meeting, and if you make it clear that the entire group bears responsibility for whatever happens, it is unlikely that you will be jumped on by the rest of the group. By making your role clear early in the meeting, you provide yourself with a precedent you can refer to if the group should forget its collective nature.

B. Nonetheless the group may attack the facilitator for a variety of reasons, the most common being the use of the facilitator as scapegoat for the failures of the group as a whole. (See p. 35.) This is potentially a constructive situation so it pays not to be defensive. Let the group vent its frustrations, even give it encouragement, but try to steer comments away from personal attacks and toward particular problems within the group. Then lead the discussion into possible solutions after all dissatisfactions have been aired and emotions have cooled. (For example, someone may attack you angrily, saying that you, the facilitator, are responsible for making this a lousy meeting. Others in the group agree, directing their remarks to you personally. Hear them through. Then, rather than trying to defend yourself or justify each of your actions, look for frustrations which you have felt with the meeting yourself. Express these, and discuss with the group how those problems might have been avoided, not just in terms of what you could have done, but also what the group as a whole might have done. Try to make the point that everyone has a responsibility to make suggestions and provide solutions to the common group problems, and that you can help this process only to the extent that others are willing to contribute and cooperate.)

C. Listen to the criticisms of your facilitation and remember them for future consideration. Facilitators are not meant to be perfect--in fact, we do most of our learning from our mistakes. Direct feedback on your role is not always easy to get, and can be valuable.

III. WHEN THERE ISN'T ENOUGH TIME TO DO WHAT YOU HAD PLANNED

A. This is the most common problem you are apt to encounter. Remember when you plan your agenda that it is easier to underestimate the amount of time needed for a section than it is to overestimate. Make allowances for this by leaving time margins in your plans. Remember to account for the fact that people may be late, that they will probably spend time chatting with each other before they will want to get down to business, and that a few will always extend the breaks beyond the scheduled amount of time.

B. If your agenda won't fit into the time you have, get the group to assign probable time limits to each section (or estimate these yourself if you are planning exercises, etc.)

C. Ask that someone in the group be responsible for keeping track of time. You may be too involved to remember to do this yourself.

D. It helps to prioritize items on an agenda, dealing with the most important ones first. This makes later curtailment much easier to handle.

E. Remind the group when time limits are being approached or exceeded. If group members want to continue in a particular area, and this will mean that something else will have to be squeezed out, make the group aware of this so they can make a decision about what to do.

F. If, halfway through the meeting, it becomes apparent that time will be short, discuss alternatives with the group, such as extending the meeting, scheduling a later one, etc.

IV. **WHEN THERE IS MORE TIME THAN YOU HAD PLANNED FOR**

A. There is nothing wrong with concluding a meeting a little early. People usually prefer this to having a session run over its time limit.

B. Don't try to cover up the extra time with mere "filler" (such as extra long discussions, unnecessary exercises, etc.). If there is something valuable to do in the time which either you or the group can suggest, by all means proceed. (It is always a good idea to prepare purposeful extra items to be used in case there is time, or in case a substitution is necessary.) On the other hand, if you simply drag out the agenda with space filler, the meeting will seem to move very slowly and will lose its sense of momentum; the extra time will be wasted or even counter-productive. Beware especially of discussions which can drag on interminably, long past the point where real information has been exchanged and repetitiousness has begun.

V. **WHEN ARGUMENTS BREAK OUT IN THE GROUP**

A. This is a difficult situation to handle, but the most important thing is to move the discussion away from personalities and toward the actual problem. Try rephrasing the comments made into general questions to the group. It is best to discourage a back-and-forth exchange between the two people and to emphasize drawing others (who are more neutral and less involved in the personal antagonisms) into the discussion. Some specific approaches you might take are:

1. Ask the rest of the group to comment on the exchange.
2. Restate the issue being discussed with the hope of clarifying it and giving a breathing space in a fast-paced discussion.
3. Focus a question toward one of the involved parties, asking for more specific reasons for a particular point of view; then ask someone else with an interest in the discussion to comment.
4. Ask each of the opponents to summarize the other's point of view. Sometimes simple misunderstandings of each other's position is at the base of an argument and by stating the opponent's beliefs, and giving the opponent the opportunity to correct any misperceptions, these misunderstandings can be cleared up.

These suggestions have the advantage of stopping a one-to-one interchange without shifting the topic off the area of disagreement. This is desirable because other members of the group may have an interest in what is going on, but have no chance to enter into the discussion, and because it is best to deal with disagreements openly rather than arbitrarily sweeping them away (assuming this does not involve spending undue time on a subject that is only of interest to a couple of people). Disagreements that are not resolved create frustrations and tend to reoccur later in more virulent form. Serious arguments that are resolved, however, sometimes move the group along significantly. (See Conflict Resolution p. 43, Crisis Intervention p. 47, and Problem Solving, p. 48.)

B. The seating arrangement can have a subtle effect on this kind of situation. The best set-up would be for the sparring partners to be seated next to each other with the facilitator directly across from both people. This is admittedly hard to accomplish, but might occur during a recess after which people are encouraged to come back to different seats (thus the advantage of informal seating in any session). It is generally best for the facilitator to avoid sitting next to either antagonist, or anyone with whom you may be interacting strongly.[1] (See Seating Arrangement, p. 15.)

C. Not infrequently, there is someone in the group who seems excessively argumentative, picking minor points in the discussion as opportunities to challenge other people or to engage in lengthy debate. It is quite easy to see how such an individual may become annoying to group members who want to proceed on to other things. So when somebody repeatedly bogs down discussion in petty argument, appeal to the other members of the group as to whether they want to continue the argument or move on. Cutting the person off yourself may be more efficient, but if done repeatedly may cause the person to resent you. By encouraging others to express their wishes, you can reinforce control of the group by its members.

VI. WHEN NOT ENOUGH OR TOO MANY PEOPLE SHOW UP

A. How many people are "too many" or "too few" is a question of the particular situation (see p. 33.) If the group is larger than 15, it generally is difficult to have discussions in which everyone can participate. Exercises often become unwieldy in such a large group as well.

B. You should prepare for the possibility of a larger or smaller group than you anticipate by selecting activites that can be modified according to the size of the group, or by having alternate activities in mind. When you plan your agenda provide leeway for flexibility in the amount of discussion time, especially if there is doubt as to the size of the group.

C. When a group is too large (or when there is a clear division in members' interests) you may want to divide the group into smaller discussion groups. This is one circumstance where it is especially convenient to have two facilitators. If you are facilitating alone, you can rove from one group to another, or you can get volunteers from the group to facilitate the smaller sections.

D. Having a smaller group than anticipated is more of a psycho-
    logical than a real hindrance. A small group can proceed
    to do quite well what a larger group was expected to do.
    But if those who did come exhibit disappointment about the
    low turnout, it is good to emphasize the positive aspects
    of the situation to bring people's spirits back up. Start
    the session with a brief discussion of the reasons for the
    low turnout, point out what the group still can accomplish,
    and reaffirm everyone's intentions of continuing anyway.
    (Or, alternatively, decide as a group to wait for a better
    time to have the meeting.)

E. If the group turns out to be quite small, you can work with
    a much looser structure (although structure should not be
    abandoned entirely). You will be able to be more flexible
    and informal and participants will be able to interact on
    a more personal level.

VII. WHEN FACILITIES AREN'T GOOD FOR WHAT YOU ARE DOING

A. (Something was said about an ounce of prevention . . . .)
    Again, it is well to prepare for this contingency in advance
    by finding out what the facilities will be, or better still,
    visiting them yourself. If another person is making the
    arrangements, make it clear what you will need in the way
    of equipment, space, and furniture.

B. If you show up and things still are not what you expected,
    consider the options available. Can the furniture be moved
    around? Can you move to a different location (out-of-doors,
    somebody's home, etc.)?

C. Ask the group's suggestions about specific problems such as
    no kitchen facilities, no movie projector, etc. Can your
    agenda be revised in such a way that you can still meet the
    group's goals for the meeting in the present situation? If
    not, are people still interested in sticking it out with
    modified plans?

VIII. WHAT DO YOU DO ABOUT YOUR OWN FEELINGS?

While you will usually not find your own feelings to be a problem (more likely they will be an asset: the facilitator is not,
nor could be, a detached observer of everything that is going
on) there may be occasions when you will be tempted to dominate the proceedings with your own feelings. Since the facilitator is in more of a position to talk freely and exert
control than other members of the group, you should be careful
that your own feelings and viewpoints are not the only ones
being discussed by the group. Monitor the discussion to see
if other people's reactions are being elicited and responded
to. When group members speak, are they addressing their comments primarily to you, or do they include the whole group?
The inexperienced facilitator is expecially prone to being too
active, feeling that he or she must respond to every little

hitch in the proceedings with a comment or suggestion. Be
patient and give things a chance to work themselves out before you take action.

IX. VOYEURS AND FLASHERS

It may be the specific purpose of a group to bring out the
emotional life of its participants and to engage in self-
revelations and emotional confrontations between members (as
in a consciousness-raising group). However, if the purpose
of the session is to exchange information, develop priorities,
or some other cognitive or practical goal, unnecessary emphasis on emotional revelation can detract from the aims of
the session. If an emotional situation arises as a product
of group interaction it should, of course, be dealt with.
But revelation for revelation's sake should be avoided. Occasionally someone will attend a cognitive workshop with the
expectation of following sensitivity group procedures and
will emphasize dramatic emotional displays and will pressure
other participants to do the same. If you become aware that
a participant is detracting from the real purpose of the
group in this way, try to gently get things back on track by
pointing out that time is being lost, or by checking out with
the rest of the group what kind of subject matter they want
to emphasize. It is a good idea to have a private conversation with the person in question when a break in the session
allows it. Point out that the individual seems to have different expectations of the session than the other members of
the group and is causing a distraction.

If the problem involves a number of people wanting to follow
sensitivity-group procedures, while a good portion of the
group does not, it would be necessary to have a group discussion clarifying participants' needs and expectations and deciding what to emphasize in the session.

X. WHEN AN EXERCISE FLOPS

A. There are two ways for an exercise to flop: when the
exercise simply doesn't proceed the way it was supposed
to; and when it does proceed as it should, but the group
misses the point of the whole thing. If you know the
exercise well (and you should!) you might realize that
faulty instructions, apathetic participation, or some
external factor is at fault. Recognizing this, you can
provide some insight to the group.

B. When you realize that an exercise flops, the first thing
to do is admit it. Point out where your expectations
were shot down, find out how others reacted, and discuss
why this occurred. Talk about what could have happened.
Such a discussion may, in itself, provide worthwhile information. Don't try to double talk your way out of a
floppy situation or find significance where there is
none. Others will sense your lack of honesty and may
be discouraged from being sincere themselves.

C. Be prepared to switch to something completely different. Hopefully, all the exercises you have prepared are not of the same type. The response to another activity may be completely different.

D. It could be that the roles played by various individuals were poorly assigned. Allow people to do what they would most like to do; their effort and imagination will be greater in such a case.

XI. WHEN SOME PARTICIPANTS CAUSE INTERRUPTIONS

A. One kind of interruption is when a participant has a tendency to cut off the current speaker with a comment of his or her own, or detracts from what the group is doing by leading the conversation to an irrelevant topic. Usually, if you diplomatically point out what is happening, the problem will be remedied. However, if the interruptions are occurring in a fast-paced, emotional discussion, some more definite measures may be needed. Suggesting a minute of silence may be enough to cool things off; so may asking people to talk slowly. A classic technique is to use some object, such as a coin, which is passed from speaker to speaker, and only the person with the object in hand is allowed to speak.

B. Another sort of interruption is caused by people getting up to go to the bathroom, get a drink of water, etc., which, depending on the circumstances, can be very distracting. Having scheduled breaks in the session will minimize this problem, unless the interruption represents boredom or dissatisfaction. (Refer to p. 59 in handling this active kind of non-participation.)

XII. MISTAKEN EXPECTATIONS - WHEN YOU HAVE BEEN MISREPRESENTED TO THE GROUP, OR THE GROUP TO YOU

A. You have been misrepresented to the group:

1. We assume that during your negotiations with the group, or its representatives, you will have clarified what your function will be and what the group expects of of you, but there is always the possibility of faulty communication somewhere in the procedure. When you get together with a new group one of the first things you should do is explain clearly what you feel your role is and what you plan to do. Hopefully, any misconceptions on the group's part or your own will be cleared up at this point, but not necessarily. False expectations can be remarkably tenacious.

2. Try to look for signs of mistaken expectations. Are questions being addressed to you about matters on which you have no expertise? Do people look to you for approval at every step? Are people unduly reluctant to give suggestions or participate? Do participants seem confused or resistant to what you are trying to do? Does it seem that you and the rest of the group are going in different directions? If there are signs that the group is expecting something other than what it is getting you should immediately bring your suspecions into the open so the group can clarify what they thought they were getting into. Hopefully, either the group will be willing to accept something different than what they had expected, or you will be able to modify your own plans, or both.

B. <u>The group has been misrepresented to you</u>. After working with a group for a short while, you may become aware that you didn't really know what you were getting into. At this point, you have three options:

1. You need more information from the group in order to do a good job of facilitating the rest of the session. .The group has, for instance, different problems than the ones you had expected, but you need to know more about these before you plan accordingly. Be open about the situation, since acquiring needed information will require either time out of the agenda, or delaying the meeting until after you can do more homework. Taking time out to gather information does not <u>always</u> have to detract from the meeting's purpose. Sometimes a group can profit in its own understanding by defining itself for an objective outsider.

2. There may be occasions when you don't think you can continue to facilitate or function in the group and must drastically change your role. (For example, you are a committed feminist and had been told you would be working with a "women's group"; and the group turns out to be a committee to lobby against the ERA.) In such a situation, it would not be fair to either simply walk out or to pretend that no conflict existed. It would be best to explain your viewpoint and what you can or cannot do with the group. If an accommodation can be reached at all, it will be through an honest discussion.

3. You may decide to say nothing. Sometimes you will be surprised by what you find in a group (e.g., they turn out to be a lot more disorganized and unstructured than you expected), but if you can see for your-

self how the group is different from your expectations, there will be little point in taking up group time discussing how and why your preconceptions proved wrong. Simply modify your plans according to the new situation as best you can. This situation is one you will probably experience sooner or later since you will never really know what to expect of an unfamiliar group until you have actually worked with it.

XIII. YOUR MATERIAL IS TOO SIMPLE OR TOO COMPLEX FOR THE GROUP

If what you are saying is too simple for the group, boredom will result. If what you are saying is too complex, you can expect confusion and blank looks. Unfortunately, blank looks and boredom look remarkably alike, so it is not always easy to figure out which problem you are dealing with.

Try to be sensitive to how the group is responding to material you use and be prepared to adapt to their level. Following are some things that will help you be alert to the group's level of comprehension.

A. Ask before doing an exercise if members of the group have ever done anything similar.

B. Begin a session by asking for some history of the group's previous experience, if for some reason you do not already know this.

C. Stop occasionally and ask if the group understands what you are doing.

D. Define any terms you may use in a specialized sense such as "evaluation" or "group process." Avoid using facilitator jargon.

E. Make sure everyone is following you. Responses from the same few people may mean that the rest of the group is far behind or far ahead.

F. If participants are moving at your speed, you can generally see it in their faces and in their level of participation. Nodding heads, interested expressions, occasional questions or comments, are good signs.

G. The type of question asked is the best indicator of what the level of comprehension is. People asking you to repeat what you just said, or questions about the terms you are using, are signs that you are on too complex a level. Questions that are surprisingly knowledgeable, showing familiarity with what you are just introducing, or incorporating points or terms which you have not yet used, are signals that you are on too simple a level.

H. If only one person is having difficulty comprehending
    what is happening, or is puzzling over one particular
    point when the rest of the group is satisfied (you might
    check this out with the group to make sure your impres-
    sion is correct) do not take an excessive amount of time
    dealing with the one person during group time. Don't
    callously brush the person off, but suggest that since
    the rest of the group is ready to move on, the two of
    you can discuss the subject more during a break or after
    the meeting.

    In the same light, don't leave the rest of the group far
    behind while you have an exclusive interchange with one
    or two members of the group whose sophistication in a
    certain area is ahead of the others'. Suggest that you
    return to a discussion that the whole group can partici-
    pate in.

XIV. SOMEONE "FREAKS OUT"

There are many reasons why a group member might have a sudden,
uncontrollable emotional outburst. The individual may feel
rejected, anxious about a personal problem brought out by a
group exercise, or disturbed by something that has been expressed in the group. Unlike other potentially lengthy interruptions which threaten a group, the "freak out" cannot be
adroitly sidestepped, contained, or delayed until after the
meeting. Since the emotions expressed are strong and important ones, they change the whole atmosphere of the meeting
and require immediate recognition and response. Of course
the actual problem that causes the outburst (whether it be
a serious psychological disturbance or a temporary anxiety)
cannot be "solved" on the spot. The immediate need is to
deal with the urgent feelings being expressed.

A. The first thing to remember is to stay calm. If the
    facilitator is relaxed and in control, but expresses
    sincere concern, it will go a long way to making the
    atmosphere in the group that of dealing with one mem-
    ber's urgent emotional expression rather than that of
    an "exciting emergency."

B. The other members of the group, unless they are threat-
    ened or frightened by the outburst, will probably be
    concerned and will feel sympathy for the person who is
    freaking out. However they may be too embarrassed or
    uncomfortable in the situation to express their sympathy
    and support. Awareness of support from other group
    members will probably be helpful to the person with the
    problem during the outburst, and will let him or her
    feel more comfortable in the group after it is over.
    Don't openly elicit expression of sympathy from others,
    since this may cause even more embarrassment or dis-
    comfort, but allow room for other people to communi-

cate their concern to the individual with the problem. In other words, you should not take command of the situation and brush others aside. You should respond immediately to the needs of the person in question, leaving room for others to help too. Sometimes there may be someone in the group, a friend, or someone with an intuitive understanding of the person's needs, who will be able to help better than you. Let them.

C. This is one situation where your concern will be more with the needs of one individual than with the group as a whole. The group should understand if you step out of your role for a minute and "abandon" them. You may say something like, "My concern right now is with David," and then turn your attention specifically to David.

D. In speaking to the person who is having the outburst, trust your intuition. How you act toward the person, what you say, or what you don't say will be a spontaneous response to the immediate situation. Basically, don't try to minimize the problem or pretend that it is not serious. Recognize that the person is experiencing intense feelings and be accepting of that. Encourage the person to air all of the most urgent feelings until he or she is able to begin to calm down naturally.

E. In some instances the subject of the outburst will be a private matter and most of the group will not be involved. In this case, the group should go on with an activity or take a break, if the incident has caused a major disruption in the activity. If the person who is upset wishes to leave the room, see if he or she wants you or another person to come along.

F. On other occasions, the incident will involve the whole group (such as when the outburst is a product of unresolved conflict in the group, or the individual's feeling rejected by the group). In this case, the individual may not withdraw from the group to deal with the feelings. The incident may be considered part of the process of the group. Your role will still be to give the person your full attention (or allow another participant to do so, if this seems appropriate) as long as seems necessary. As the person with the problem begins to calm down, start to involve other members of the group, and encourage members to deal with the incident as a group experience.

G. At some point, it will be time to return to the original focus of the meeting. When you judge that it is time to do this, ask the person(s) involved if they feel ready to go on. Accept that what has happened has affected the group (i.e., don't act as if nothing happened at all), but don't dwell on it after it is over. Treat the outburst as an intense, but natural venting of feelings and go on from there. (If the group has trouble settling down to business at this point, it may be a good time for a short break.)

H. If the freaking out is treated as a private matter and dealt with apart from the group, participants may not have dealt with their own reactions to the episode and a short discussion of how the group has been affected may be necessary before going back to business.

XV. SUMMARY

Following are some simple principles that are good to keep in mind in preventing problems or dealing with problems that do occur.

A. Adequate preparation for a group is the best safeguard against serious problems.

B. Make sure you know what the group expects of you, and let them know what you expect of the group.

C. Be flexible in your planning; have alternate sequences of items on your agenda, and substitutions in mind.

D. Don't be too serious when you confront a problem. A little humor can make the situation much easier to handle.

E. Make sure you have an understanding with the group: they share the responsibility for the meeting. They are free to criticize and are responsible for letting the facilitator know what is going on and what their reactions are.

F. Be honest with the group at all times.

G. Try to anticipate problems you might have. Catching them early has many advantages.

Appendix A

FINDING FACILITATION TRAINING COURSES

A wide variety of educational programs fall into the category of facilitator training. Group process, human relations and leadership skills are all much-used descriptions to look for. Sponsorship and cost is also very diverse. Workshops can usually be found associated with in-service training for many professions, with university course offerings, or with some social action groups.

We are not comfortable making specific recommendations for you, since your own special interests, values, and ability to pay will be factors in your choice. Check out your options. Talk with associates, with people who have been involved in the training program you are interested in, and with whoever is sponsoring it. One thing to watch for is that "facilitation" courses can range along a continuum from group process skills to therapy techniques. Make sure the program you are getting into stresses the skills you want to learn. We hope that a thorough assessment will spare you from wasting your time in a program that doesn't meet your expectations or needs.

The Center for Conflict Resolution has provided training in meeting skills, group process and facilitation to various groups as well as occasionally conducting training workshops open to the public. We welcome inquiries from interested parties. We urge those who are interested in CCR's services (or any kind of training) to compare programs and evaluate how well they meet your own needs according to the criteria mentioned above. Some background information on CCR can be found in the "Preface" on page ix.

DON'T WASTE THIS SPACE
WRITE SOME NOTES HERE

Appendix B

SAMPLE AGENDAS

Following are two agendas which were developed and used by the authors in workshop situations.

I. WORKSHOP AT THE YWCA:

A. The situation: CCR was asked to present a 1½ - 2 hour workshop on conflict resolution that was to be part of an all-day "round robin" program in which participants attended three workshops at intervals during the day. For each time slot participants had the choice of several workshops that they could attend. We asked for the time slot right after lunch since previous experience had demonstrated that by the final workshop of the day, participants were tired and had low energy levels.

B. The group: The program was being offered as a final event in a training program for individuals who were going to be facilitating actualization groups of adolescents in the middle schools. Most of the participants were graduate students in social work, or had a similar background. While many members would not know each other, they had similar values, interests and informational backgrounds. We could expect somewhere from 5 to 15 participants.

C. Our goals: We decided to try to present some basic information about conflict resolution in ways that participants could apply to the situations they would be dealing with. We were especially interested in motivating the participants to identify with the adolescents they would be working with and to try to understand their perspectives. We expected that most of the participants would be fairly sophisticated in their ability to work with conflict resolution theories and would be able to pick up ideas quickly and discuss and apply them. However, since we had only two hours, we could plan to do no more than skim the surface of the subject.

D. The agenda (as planned):

1. Ask group members to introduce themselves to us and each other and tell a little bit about their backgrounds in areas that would interest the rest of the group. Introduce ourselves as individuals and as representatives of CCR and describe what kind of organization CCR is.

2. Ask group members to explain to us the school program in which they will be participating. This will clarify any misunderstandings that we may have and give us an idea of what the program means to the participants so that we can better relate the workshop to their interests, values and needs.

3. Facilitators will describe workshop plans so that group members will know what to expect, and will have a chance to suggest changes if they have a reason. Describe what role we see ourselves as playing in the group and the kind of participation we expect from others.

4. Ask each group member to describe some kind of conflict she or he anticipates having to deal with in the program. Write list on newsprint for everyone to see. This will encourage group members to share their thoughts, promote discussion, allow the facilitators to know the specific interests and needs of the group, and provide some specific conflict examples to apply our theoretical ideas to.

5. Ask the group to select one of the anticipated conflicts on the list and ask each participant to write down (in a minute or so) a brief description of how she or he would deal with that conflict. Everyone will then be asked to read her or his solution, which will also be written on newsprint. The purpose of this activity is to demonstrate the wide variety of solutions that exist, and to allow participants to talk with each other, share ideas, and use each other as resource people. This information could also be used as demonstration material to apply theoretical information to.

   Repeat this step once or twice according to the amount of time available and how interested participants appear to be.

6. A short lecture by one of the facilitators, accompanied by a handout, on styles of conflict behavior. Sample solutions from the previous step in the agenda will be used to demonstrate these different styles. Group opinions will be elicited on the kinds of situations in which each of these styles might be appropriate or inappropriate. (This step will present information, relate that information to the specific needs and interests of the group, and get group members to think about the information and exchange ideas about it.)

7. A lecturette, by the other facilitator, on group techniques for problem solving. A group discussion in which participants suggest ways different tech-

niques might be used in the situations already described. Again, the purpose is to present information and to get participants to relate that information to their own needs.

8. Make group decision on which of four activities to include. (Consider the interests and energy levels of the participants and amount of time available.)

   a. Continue the group discussion in relation to the list of conflicts generated in Step 4. Ask people to use the information presented in Steps 6 and 7 to suggest ways of dealing with these conflicts, and encourage them to discuss the values involved with conflict resolution in their situations.

   b. Have the group do role plays on potential conflict situations and discuss their feelings and ideas using the conflict resolution information presented previously. The role plays can encourage them to identify with the adolescents they will be working with.

   c. Discuss the use of exercises in groups. Do one exercise in the group which involves a short role play that demonstrates different styles of group interaction. Then discuss some values and techniques of using exercises in groups and describe some of the exercises that we have found useful. This will provide participants with tools that they can take back to their own groups.

   d. Do the Ugli Orange Exercise. This is a long role play that involves a conflict situation and relates very demonstratably to the information provided in Steps 6 and 7.

9. Have a summary in which we answer any questions that participants have about earlier parts of the session and allow any further discussion that group members are interested in continuing. Then ask for feedback and request that participants fill out a short evaluation form of 3 or 4 open-ended questions. This will finish the session off without dangling ends or unfulfilled expectations, and allow the facilitators to know how satisfied the participants are and how well we have met their needs.

E. How the workshop actually went. The workshop went well. Since the participants themselves had been trained as facilitators, their expectations of our role in the group were quite similar to our own. They took a great deal of responsibility for group process and were enthusiastic about group discussion. However, there were some changes in the agenda and there was not enough time to do everything we had planned.

1. During Step 4, one of the group members asked for a definition of "conflict." We had not planned to deal with this in the agenda because we usually assume that a conflict is occurring whenever someone perceives that to be the case. However, since group members seemed interested in discussing this question, we took time out to do that. This led to one of the facilitators presenting a list of some of the different kinds of conflict that can occur, for participants to use in analyzing future conflict situations.

2. Because of the above, and because group discussion took longer than we had planned, we eliminated Step 8 altogether. Most of our basic information and discussion had already been presented and the alternatives planned for Step 8 were mostly ways of elaborating or reviewing this information. Since several group members showed interest in the theoretical information we were presenting, we took a few minutes to run quickly through a list of conditions in groups that facilitate problem solving for members to consider on their own time, although there was no time for discussion of these points.

3. We did not have time for as long a summary and evaluation period as we had hoped. Since group participation had been very high and members were vocal about expressing their interests and opinions throughout the session, we did not feel too badly about this. We hope that most things were cleared up in the process of the meeting. However, cutting this section short is still regrettable. The person who had arranged for us to do the workshop provided us with evaluation forms that she wished to use for her own records, and since we were allowed access to this information, we did not use our own evaluation questions.

II. WORKSHOP AT AN "ALTERNATIVES" CONFERENCE

Unlike the previous workshop, which was part of a training program for people going into a certain vocation, the following workshop was a skills sharing session for people who were already working in a common field. In this instance, the facilitators did not play the role of primary resource people for the group, but acted in the capacity of helping group members to be resource people for each other. For this reason, we went into the workshop with a much less defined agenda so that the workshop could adapt to the specific interests of the individuals participating.

A. The situation: The workshop occurred at a three-day conference on alternatives to drug abuse, attended by alcohol and other drug abuse educators. It was a two-hour, morning session, with a very informal atmosphere. The subject was "community decision making."

B. <u>The group</u>: There were 15 individuals in various roles from alcohol and drug abuse education agencies all over Wisconsin. The facilitators were a CCR staff member with drug abuse prevention experience and the state drug abuse prevention coordinator from Oregon.

C. <u>Our goals</u>: We wanted to generate discussion and information sharing on community decision making--what it is, is it valuable? If so, how to help it happen.

D. <u>The agenda (as planned)</u>.

1. Introduction of facilitators and other participants. Since we will not all know each other, share information on each individual's type of work and reason for interest in the workshop.

2. Give each participant an index card and ask members to write a definition of community decision making and give an example. Then have the group read the definitions out loud. A facilitator will write this information on newsprint for everyone to see and discuss. Get participants to exchange reactions, discuss values and costs of community decision making.

3. Discuss "How do we do it?" A short lecture, with handouts, by one of the facilitators. The lecture will refer to ideas from Step 2 for illustration.

4. Discuss obstacles to community decision making. Get the group to define and trace obstacles.

5. Select the most pervasive obstacle(s) and discuss their causes and cures.

6. A summary lecturette by one of the facilitators.

7. Evaluation.

E. <u>How the workshop actually went</u>. Those who attended were all strongly committed to the idea of community decision making and there was a unanimous assumption that it was desirable. There was a certain amount of frustration, though, on the part of those who were trying to make community decision making work in their own communities, and the discussion focused primarily on problems.

1. During Step 4, the group quickly agreed that lack of participation was the primary obstacle to community decision making. The facilitators had the group do a <u>web chart</u> on this problem. ("Lack of participation" was written in the center of a blackboard. The group brainstormed a list of causes for this problem which

were written around the periphery of the board. Then the group discussed relationships between the causes and connected the related causes with lines on the board. The purpose of this activity was to break down the problem into parts, and discover how those parts related to each other.)

2. This activity led to a long discussion of the problems that one specific agency was having. This appeared to be a digression from the agenda, but since the group was interested in the discussion, and since it involved analyzing the situation in a way that related to the problems of other agencies, we felt the discussion was worthwhile.

3. Issues that we felt were important were raised in this workshop, although we would have liked to have gone farther in our sharing of strategies for implementation. During the evaluation, participants said they were pleased with the perspective that the workshop had given them. Some commented that they felt our discussion had made the values and appropriate strategies much more explicit. People clearly picked up ideas from one another.

Appendix C

THE UGLI ORANGE EXERCISE

This Ugli Orange Exercise is a role play that simulates a conflict situation. We have found it very useful for stimulating discussion of conflict behavior and factors affecting conflict. There are a number of exercises that can be used for this purpose, and we hope you will not get in the rut of always using just one. However, we are including this exercise here because it is not readily available in any other publications.

I. <u>TRAINER INSTRUCTIONS</u>

A. Have the participants break into groups of two.

B. Hand out printed role instructions, one each per group.

C. Say, "I am the owner of the remaining Ugli oranges. After you read about your roles, spend about 6 to 10 minutes meeting with the other firm's representative and decide on a course of action. I am strictly interested in making a profit and will sell my oranges to the highest bidder. Since my country is alien to yours, there is no way either government will assist you in obtaining the oranges from me. Each pair of negotiators can assume that there are no others interested in the oranges.

"When you have reached a decision, pick a spokesperson who will tell me:

1. What do you plan to do?

2. If you want to buy the oranges, what price will you offer?

3. To whom and how will the oranges be delivered?"

D. Stop the exercise after about half the groups have reached a solution. In the discussion, pay particular attention to those groups who have not reached agreement. What were the issues there? Were they withholding or disclosing information? What was the trust level?

E. Post the following column headings and write information from different groups under them:

1. Was there full disclosure? (What information was shared?) (Have a column for the "Jones" role and one for the "Roland" role.)

*Copyright R. J. House. Included here with the permission of the author.

81

2. Did you trust each other? (Ask them and infer from their solution.)

3. Would you work with each other again? (How satisfied were you?) (Have a column for "Jones" and a column for "Roland.")

4. How creative (or complex) was the solution? (The solution is often complex or creative when trust is low.)

F. Topics for discussion:

1. Mutual interaction of disclosure and trust. One can stimulate the other. Trust cycles.

2. Importance of identifying whether goals are compatible before deciding whether competition or co-operation is appropriate. (We often tend to assume competition when it may not be appropriate.)

3. Under mistrust, much creative energy is wasted by dreaming up ingenious strategies to screw the other, or to avoid being screwed.

II. The roles:

A. Role for Roland--Ugli Orange Case

You are Dr. P. W. Roland. You work as a research biologist for a pharmaceutical firm. The firm is under contract with the government to do research on methods to combat enemy uses of biological warfare.

Recently several World War II experimental nerve gas bombs were moved from the U.S. to a small island just off the U.S. coast in the Pacific. In the process of transporting them two of the bombs developed a leak. The leak is presently controlled but government scientists believe that the gas will permeate the bomb chambers within two weeks. They know of no method of preventing the gas from getting into the atmosphere and spreading to other islands, and very likely to the West Coast as well. If this occurs, it is likely that several thousands of people will incur serious brain damage or die.

You've developed a synthetic vapor which will neutralize the nerve gas if it is injected into the bomb chamber before the gas leaks out. The vapor is made with a chemical taken from the rind of the Ugli orange, a very rare fruit. Unfortunately, only 4000 of these oranges were produced this season.

You've been informed, on good evidence, that a Mr. R. H. Cardoza, a fruit exporter in South America, is in possession of 3000 Ugli oranges. The chemicals from the rinds of this number of oranges would be sufficient to neutralize the gas if the serum is developed and injected efficiently. You have also been informed that the rinds of these oranges are in good condition.

You have also been informed that Dr. J. W. Jones is also urgently seeking purchase of Ugli oranges and he is aware of Mr. Cardoza's possession of the 3000 available. Dr. Jones works for a firm with which your firm is highly competitive. There is a great deal of industrial espionage in the pharmaceutical industry. Over the years, your firm and Dr. Jones' firm have sued each other for violations of industrial espionage laws and infringement of patent rights several times. Litigation on two suits is still in process.

The Federal government has asked your firm for assistance. You've been authorized by your firm to approach Mr. Cardoza to purchase the 3000 Ugli oranges. You have been told he will sell them to the highest bidder. Your firm has authorized you to bid as high as $250,000 to obtain the rind of the oranges.

Before approaching Mr. Cardoza, you have decided to talk to Dr. Jones to influence him so that he will not prevent you from purchasing the oranges.

B. Role for Jones--Ugli Orange Case

You are Dr. John W. Jones, a biological research scientist employed by a pharmaceutical firm. You have recently developed a synthetic chemical useful for curing and preventing Rudosen. Rudosen is a disease contracted by pregnant women. If not caught in the first four weeks of pregnancy, the disease causes serious brain, eye, and ear damage to the unborn child. Recently, there has been an outbreak of Rudosen in your state and several thousand women have contracted the disease. You have found, with volunteer victims, that your recently developed synthetic serum cures Rudosen in its early stages. Unfortunately, the serum is made from the juice of the Ugli orange which is a very rare fruit. Only a small quantity (approximately 4000) of these oranges were produced last season. No additional Ugli oranges will be available until next season, which will be too late to cure the present Rudosen victims.

You've demonstrated that your synthetic serum is in no way harmful to pregnant women. Consequently, there are no side effects. The Food and Drug Administration has approved the production and distribution of the serum as a cure for Rudosen.

Unfortunately, the present outbreak was unexpected and your firm had not planned on having the compound serum available for six months. Your firm holds the patent on the synthetic serum and it is expected to be a highly profitable product when it is generally available to the public.

You have recently been informed, on good evidence, that Mr. R. H. Cardoza, a South American fruit exporter, is in possession of 3000 Ugli oranges in good condition. If you could obtain the juice of all 3000 you would be able to both cure the present victims and provide sufficient inoculation for the remaining pregnant women in the state. No other state currently has a Rudosen threat.

You have recently been informed that Dr. P. W. Roland is also urgently seeking Ugli oranges and is also aware of Mr. Cardoza's possession of the 3000 available. Dr. Roland is employed by a competitor pharmaceutical firm. He has been working on biological warfare research for the past several years. There is a great deal of industrial espionage in the pharmaceutical industry. Over the past several years, Dr. Roland's firm and your firm have sued each other for infringement of patent rights and espionage law violations several times.

You've been authorized by your firm to approach Mr. Cardoza to purchase the 3000 Ugli oranges. You have been told he will sell them to the highest bidder. Your firm has authorized you to bid as high as $250,000 to obtain the juice of the 3000 available oranges.

Before approaching Mr. Cardoza, you have decided to talk with Dr. Roland to influence him so that he will not prevent you from purchasing the oranges.

III. USING THE EXERCISE

A. An important factor in this role play is that one person is seeking the rinds of the oranges and the other person is seeking the juice. Usually the participants will begin the role play perceiving themselves to be in competition over the whole orange. How the role play proceeds depends on how soon (if ever) the participants realize that their needs are not necessarily mutually exclusive. Two factors affecting this are how sophisticated the participants are in understanding problem solving principles, and how much competition is perceived (which you can influence in the way you set the exercise up, what instructions you give). We have often used this exercise simply to illustrate conflict behaviors and to demonstrate what a problem solving solution might be. However, the exercise can also be used as the basis of a much more complex examination of the dynamics of competition and problem solving.

B. You can vary the way you use this exercise according to the situation and your purpose for using it. One common variation is to have a third participant observe the role play and give feedback and analysis afterwards. Another is to have the roles of Dr. Roland and Dr. Jones played by teams of two or three individuals and to re-quire a consensus decision of the group. This variation has the added comlexity of forcing participants to agree with the other members of their team as well as competing with an "adversary." Competition is often more intense in this situation.

Appendix D

SOURCES OF EXERCISES

We have intentionally included very few exercises in this manual.
The reason for this is that we think facilitators should be aware
of and able to use the many fine reference books on this subject
that already exist. It is easy to become comfortable with a few
exercises and get in the rut of using them almost exclusively. We
urge you to become familiar with many exercises, to test them, to
learn to select the ones appropriate for a particular situation,
and to adapt them accordingly. Below are some sources of exercises
which we particularly recommend. You will be able to find others
that relate to your specific area of interest.

Virginia Coover, Ellen Deacon, Charles Esser, Christopher Moore,
        Resource Manual for a Living Revolution (copies available
        from Movement for a New Society, 4722 Baltimore Avenue,
        Philadelphia, PA 19143). Very good material on organiz-
        ing for social change and using groups in working for
        change. It has a good selection of exercises. The values
        behind this resource manual are very much in line with
        the values expressed here.

Gerard Egan, Encounter: Group Process for Interpersonal Growth
        (Wadsworth: 1970). This is a book of encounter techniques,
        many of which should only be used by experienced counselors.

Theodore Grove, Experiences in Interpersonal Communication (Prentice-
        Hall: 1976). Includes exercises and introductory discussion
        in the areas of interpersonal and group communication as well
        as activities aimed at changing communication behavior.

David W. Johnson and Frank P. Johnson, Joining Together (Prentice-
        Hall: 1975). This contains information on group theory
        and group skills.

David W. Johnson, Reaching Out: Interpersonal Effectiveness and
        Self-Actualization (Prentice-Hall: 1972). This is a very
        suggestive book of techniques for developing communication
        skills.

Stephanie Judson (ed.), A Manual on Nonviolence and Children
        (Nonviolence and Children Program, Friends Peace Committee,
        1515 Cherry Street, Philadephia, PA 19102: 1977). A good
        resource for working with children. It contains accounts
        of programs on nonviolence and conflict resolution in
        various schools, as well as good theoretical and practical
        suggestions.

Eleanor Morrison and Mita Price, Values in Sexuality (Hart Publications: 1974). The main emphasis here is a new approach to sex education.

J. William Pfieffer and John E. Jones, eds., Annual Handbooks for Group Facilitators (University Associates Publishers, Inc.: since 1972). These contain new structured experiences, theoretical sections, and some lecturettes that may be helpful.

J. William Pfieffer and John E. Jones, A Handbook of Structured Experiences for Human Relations Training Vols. I, II, III and IV (University Associates Press, Iowa City: 1970). These are standard references that you can find in most libraries. They contain many exercises relating to communication, group work and decision making.

Priscilla Prutzman, Leonard Burger, Gretchen Budehamer and Lee Stern, Children's Creative Response to Conflict (Quaker Project on Community Conflict, 15 Rutherford Place, New York, NY 10003: 1977). A very complete program for building a cooperative classroom or introducing children to conflict resolution. Many activities for elementary and middle school children in the areas of self concept, communication, affirmation and conflict resolution.

Simon, Howe and Kirshenbaum, Values Clarification (Hart Publishers: 1972). Practical strategies for teachers and students can be found here. Also see other books by same authors.

Gene Stanford, Developing Effective Classroom Groups (Hart: 1977). A step-by-step plan for developing a learning group, well adapted to grades 6-12 or older. It contains many exercises.

Gene Stanford and Barbara Dodds Stanford, Learning Discussion Skills Through Games (Citation Press, NY: 1969). Includes skill-building exercises aimed at common problems in groups for high school and middle school ages.

FOOTNOTES

Chapter One

1. An immense amount of research and thinking have gone into the study of leadership. For a good introduction see "Contemporary Trends in the Analysis of Leadership Processes" by E. P. Hollander and J. W. Julian, Psychological Bulletin, 1969, 71, 387-397. This article discusses the leader-follower interaction and voices many useful points about the leadership process.

Chapter Two

1. B. M. Bass and J. A. Vaughan, Training in Industry: The Management of Learning (1966: Wadsworth). Also M. Beer, "The Technology of Organizational Development" in M. D. Dunnette (ed.) Handbook of Industrial and Organizational Psychology (1975: Rand-McNally) .

Chapter Three

1. R. Sommer, "Small Group Ecology," Psychological Bulletin, 1967, 67, 145-52; F. L. Strodtbeck and L. H. Hook, "The Social Dimension of a Twelve-Man Jury Table," Sociometry, 1961, 24, 397-415/

Chapter Four

1. Meyer, H. H., E. Kay and J. P. French, "Split Roles in Performance Appraisal," Harvard Business Review, 1965, 43 (1), 123-129.

2. See Andre Delbecq, A. VandeVen and D. Gustavson, Group Techniques for Program Planning (1975: Scott Foresman) pp. 114-115 for a discussion on question phrasing.

3. Michael Argyle, Social Interaction (1969: Aldine) pp. 222-223.

4. There are both positive and negative aspects to scapegoating. See Peter J. Burke, "Scapegoating: An Alternative to Role Differentiation," Sociometry, 1969, 32, 159-168.

Chapter Five

1. See Alan G. Filley, Interpersonal Conflict Resolution (1975: Scott Foresman) Chs. 2 and 4, for a review on styles of conflict behavior.

2. Clifford Swenson, Introduction to Interpersonal Relations (1973: Scott Foresman) pp. 272-282.

Chapter Seven

1. Alan Filley, Interpersonal Conflict Resolution, op. cit., pp. 85-87.